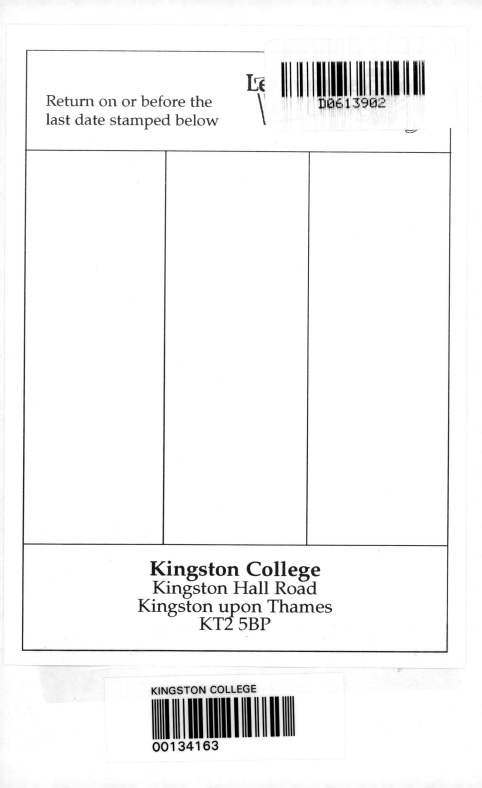

Return on or before the
last date stamped below

D0613902

Kingston College
Kingston Hall Road
Kingston upon Thames
KT2 5BP

C. Day Lewis was born in Ireland in 1904. He won scholarships to Sherborne School and Wadham College, Oxford, where he read Classics. His reputation as a poet was quickly established with *Transitional Poem* (1929) and *From Feathers to Iron* (1931) and he went on to publish many other volumes of poetry, as well as essays, critical studies and much admired translations of Virgil and Valéry. Early in his career Day Lewis supported himself and his family by schoolmastering, but in 1935 he became a full-time writer, encouraged by the success of the crime novels he wrote under the pseudonym Nicholas Blake. Like many contemporary artists and intellectuals he was strongly committed to the Communist Party in the 1930s, but in 1938 he left the party and he spent the war years working for the Ministry of Information.

After the war Day Lewis became popular as a broadcaster, lecturer and as a reader of poetry, often in partnership with his second wife, Jill Balcon. He was Clark Lecturer at Cambridge (1946), Professor of Poetry at Oxford (1951–56), Charles Eliot Norton Professor at Harvard (1964–65), and Compton Lecturer at Hull University (1968). He was also a Fellow and Vice-President of the Royal Society of Literature, Chairman of the Literature Panel at the Arts Council, a member of the Irish Academy of Letters and an honorary member of the American Academy of Arts and Letters. Day Lewis was awarded honorary doctorates by the University of Exeter and Trinity College, Dublin, and was made a Companion of Literature by the Royal Society of Literature. He was created CBE in 1951 and in 1968 was appointed Poet Laureate. He died in May 1972 and is buried near Thomas Hardy at Stinsford, Dorset.

Jill Balcon has had a distinguished broadcasting career for over sixty years. A former director of the Apollo Society, she is well known for her public readings of poetry in the UK, Europe and America. She is the editor of the *Posthumous Poems* and *The Complete Poems* of C. Day Lewis, and as an anthologist compiled *The Pity of War*. Jill Balcon is President of the Society of Teachers of Speech and Drama, and a Vice-President of the Thomas Hardy Society, the Wilfred Owen Association and The Poetry Society. Her recordings of audio-books include the award-winning *Samuel Pepys, The Unequalled Self* by Claire Tomalin, *The Aeneid of Virgil*, in C. Day Lewis's translation (with Paul Scofield and Toby Stephens), *Northanger Abbey* by Jane Austen, and *The World's Wife* by Carol Ann Duffy.

C. Day Lewis
Selected Poems

EDITED AND INTRODUCED BY JILL BALCON

ENITHARMON PRESS

First published in 2004
by the Enitharmon Press
26B Caversham Road
London NW5 2DU

www.enitharmon.co.uk

Distributed in the UK by
Central Books
99 Wallis Road
London E9 5LN

ISBN 1 904634 11 7

Enitharmon Press gratefully acknowledges the financial support of
Arts Council England, London.

British Library Cataloguing-in-Publication Data.
A catalogue record for this book is available
from the British Library.

Typeset in Caslon by Servis Filmsetting Ltd
and printed in England by
Antony Rowe Ltd

SELECT BIBLIOGRAPHY

Place of publication is London unless otherwise cited

Poetry
Beechen Vigil (Fortune Press, 1925)
Country Comets (Martin Hopkinson, 1928)
Transitional Poem (The Hogarth Press, 1929)
From Feathers to Iron (The Hogarth Press, 1931)
The Magnetic Mountain (The Hogarth Press, 1933)
Collected Poems, 1929–1933 (The Hogarth Press, 1935)
A Time to Dance and Other Poems (The Hogarth Press, 1935)
Noah and the Waters (The Hogarth Press, 1936)
Overtures to Death and Other Poems (Jonathan Cape, 1938)
Poems in Wartime (Jonathan Cape, 1940)
Word Over All (Jonathan Cape, 1943)
Poems 1943–1947 (Jonathan Cape, 1948)
Collected Poems, 1929–1936 (The Hogarth Press, 1948)
Selected Poems (Harmondsworth: Penguin Books, 1951, 1957, 1969)
An Italian Visit (Jonathan Cape, 1953)
Collected Poems (Jonathan Cape/The Hogarth Press, 1954)
Pegasus and Other Poems (Jonathan Cape, 1957)
The Gate and Other Poems (Jonathan Cape, 1962)
Requiem for the Living (New York: Harper & Row, 1964)
The Room and Other Poems (Jonathan Cape, 1965)
The Whispering Roots (Jonathan Cape, 1970)
Posthumous Poems (Andoversford: The Whittington Press, 1979)
The Complete Poems (Sinclair-Stevenson, 1992)

5

Non-fiction
A Hope for Poetry (Oxford: Basil Blackwell, 1934)
The Poetic Image (Jonathan Cape, 1947)
The Lyrical Poetry of Thomas Hardy (Geoffrey Cumberlege, 1953)
Notable Images of Virtue: Emily Brontë, George Meredith, W. B. Yeats (Toronto: The Ryerson Press, 1954)
The Buried Day (autobiography; Chatto and Windus, 1960)
The Lyric Impulse (Chatto and Windus/Cambridge, MA: Harvard University Press, 1965)
A Need for Poetry? (Hull: University of Hull, 1968)

Translations
The Georgics of Virgil (Jonathan Cape, 1940)
Paul Valéry, *Le Cimetière marin/The Graveyard by the Sea* (Secker and Warburg, 1947)
The Aeneid of Virgil (The Hogarth Press, 1952)
The Eclogues of Virgil (Jonathan Cape, 1963)

Fiction (as Nicholas Blake)
20 crime novels, from *A Question of Proof* (1935) to *The Private Wound* (1968)

Editor
[with W. H. Auden] *Oxford Poetry* (Oxford: Basil Blackwell, 1927)
The Mind in Chains: Socialism and the Cultural Revolution (Frederick Muller, 1937)
Wilfred Owen, *Collected Poems* (Chatto and Windus, 1963)

CONTENTS

From *An Italian Visit* (1953)

From *Pegasus and Other Poems* (1957)

From *The Gate and Other Poems* (1962)

Dedicated
with my love
to these three 'Guardians'

David Whiting, Graham Johnson & Stephen Stuart-Smith

J.B.
April 2004

INTRODUCTION

In C. Day Lewis's centenary year it is heartening to be able to introduce a substantial *Selected Poems*. This volume is largely based on the selection he made for Penguin in 1951, which he extended in 1957 and 1969. To these poems I have added particular favourites from the collections published in his lifetime, together with some of the *Posthumous Poems* and a few *vers d'occasion*: as Poet Laureate he wrote a number, always on subjects that were important to him and of significance in the world – famine, flood, libraries, to name a few.

I shall now call him Cecil, though at his insistence his Christian name, which he disliked, was never printed after 1927, except in ignorance.

In his preface to the *Collected Poems 1954* he wrote, after rereading them:

> I have felt both surprise and regret: regret, that so much energy should so often have run to waste; surprise to hear a buried self speaking, now and then, with such urgency. Some poets can rewrite and improve their early work, years later. I wish I could do so; but the selves who wrote those poems are strangers to me, and I cannot resume their identities or go back into the world where they lived. There are certain themes, no doubt, linking these dead selves together. Perhaps these constant themes compose the personal tradition of a poet – his one continuity, defining and preserving, through every change of language, every change of heart, what is essential to him . . .

EDITOR'S NOTE: Much of this introduction was written for inclusion in *The Complete Poems*. Where I have referred to poems not included in this new *Selected Poems*, their titles are marked with an asterisk.

It might be helpful to remind today's readers of some of the facts comprehensively documented elsewhere. The 'Macspaunday' poets who flowered in the 'thirties (C. Day Lewis, W. H. Auden, Louis MacNeice, Stephen Spender) were friends, but never a group. They had shared the same privileged background, public school and Oxford – in Cecil's case through scholarships and exhibitions, as his father was a parson of no means. However, adolescent life in his father's Nottinghamshire mining parish also included tennis parties in 'the Dukeries' and he became acutely aware of the contrast between the lowest and highest strata of society. In his poem, 'Sketches for a Self-Portrait' (*Poems 1943–1947*) he

> looked for a lost ball
> In the laurels, they smirched with pit-grime . . .

He had seen his father sitting by the bedsides of miners coughing themselves to death. His outrage at social injustice stemmed from that time. Then, with the onset of fascism and the Spanish Civil War, came the urgent wish to prevent war. For the time being he turned to communism along with many other artists and intellectuals of this period.

The late Clifford Dyment, in his booklet *C. Day Lewis* (1955), thought that the poetic powers of the author of the so-called 'Political' poems could carry the reader over the rough places and sometimes didactic tone 'by the beauty and momentum of the verse itself'. Cecil was a man with music in his bones (he had a ravishing light tenor singing voice, and was one of the finest speakers of verse of his generation – accomplishments not universal among poets). Stanzas from these love poems of the 'Political' period show his lyricism.

> . . . Desire is a witch
> And runs against the clock.
> It can unstitch
> The decent hem
> Where space tacks on to time:
> It can unlock
> Pandora's privacies . . .
>
> *Transitional Poem*

13

... With me, my lover makes
The clock assert its chime:
But when she goes, she takes
The mainspring out of time ...
Transitional Poem

... Beauty's end is in sight,
Terminus where all feather joys alight.
Wings that flew lightly
Fold and are iron. We see
The thin end of mortality ...
From Feathers to Iron

... Do not expect again a phoenix hour,
The triple-towered sky, the dove complaining,
Sudden the rain of gold and heart's first ease
Tranced under trees by the eldritch light of sundown ...
From Feathers to Iron

Those early love lyrics nearly cost him his job at Cheltenham Junior School. In his autobiography *The Buried Day* he tells how the head-master had seen *Transitional Poem* in the local bookshop and summoned Cecil to his study. H.M. was clearly deeply embarrassed, and asked C. if he thought he was fit to teach little boys, because the poems were ... (he couldn't bring himself to say it) 'extremely ... excessively ... er ... SEXUAL'. 'But they're love poems,' blurted out Cecil, 'addressed to my wife.'

As a schoolmaster, and later as a professor, Cecil insisted that one must respond to a poem directly, spontaneously, positively – 'to be able to enjoy before we can learn to discriminate'. He also said: 'Modern poetry is every poem, whether written last year or five centuries ago, that has meaning for us still.' The reader will find some themes prevailing throughout his work: hero-worship, fear, compassion, transience, very often the conflict of a divided heart and mind, and always the relentless compulsion to know himself.

Cecil was a modest man; I wish to make no extravagant claims on his behalf. He himself thought that only his sonnet sequence 'O

Dreams, O Destinations' (*Word Over All*) might, possibly, endure. At the end of his life, when asked to contribute to James Gibson's anthology *Let the Poet Choose*, he submitted the last of those nine sonnets, and 'On Not Saying Everything' (*The Room*) which he wrote during a fruitful time at Harvard in 1964–5, when he held the Charles Eliot Norton Chair. This is what he said: 'May I suggest . . . the sonnet because, though I wrote it 30 years ago, it still stands up and says something I feel to be truthful about the human condition: "On not saying everything" because I believe so strongly in the doctrine of limitations it speaks for – that everything, a tree, a poem, a human relationship, lives and thrives by the limits imposed on it.'

Of course poets are not always their own best judges. However, in their solitude, they cannot realise how much and where they touch other people's lives. I am touched myself when friends, and often strangers, quote passages of Cecil's which move them and, moreover, sustain them. 'Walking Away' (*The Gate*) usually brings many reactions whenever it is broadcast or read in public.

> . . . I have had worse partings, but none that so
> Gnaws at my mind still. Perhaps it is roughly
> Saying what God alone could perfectly show –
> How selfhood begins with a walking away,
> And love is proved in the letting go.

Anyone who has lost a child, or simply left one at the new school gate, can identify with the parting. 'My Mother's Sister' (*The Room*) is a poignant poem about the beloved aunt who brought him up from the age of four when his mother died. In both these poems he avoids sentimentality – a real achievement. It is interesting that religious images appear often in Cecil's poems, even though he became a rather 'churchy' agnostic after the years of living in a parsonage. The title poem in *The Gate* was dedicated to Trekkie Parsons. One week-end in her house, he couldn't take his eyes off a picture she had painted. I could see it was saying something to him, and thanks to her generosity I bought it for him in instalments.

15

. . . We expect nothing (the flowers might add), we only
Await: this pure awaiting –
It is the kind of worship we are taught.

It was greatly encouraging to Cecil that Henry Moore, after reading
a typescript of 'The Expulsion' (*Posthumous Poems*), told him he had
learned something new about the fresco by Masaccio which had
inspired the poem. Only recently – I wish I could tell the author –
that superb pianist and scholar Graham Johnson said to me that
'Cornet Solo' (*Word Over All*) was 'the most evocative poem I know
about the power of music in childhood's memory.'

. . . Strange how those yearning airs could sweeten
And still enlighten
The hours when solitude gave me her breast.
Strange they could tell a mere child how hearts may beat in
The self-same tune for the once-possessed
And the unpossessed . . .

Adverse academic criticism could not demolish these statements of
faith by other artists.

Some of those who declared that CDL 'had no voice of his own'
had not, perhaps, listened or looked carefully enough. This is what
he said himself about influences: 'I myself have been technically
influenced, and enabled to clarify my thoughts, by such diverse
poets as Yeats, Wordsworth, Robert Frost, Virgil, Valéry, W. H.
Auden, and Hardy. They suggested to me ways of saying what I had
to say. Any given poem thus influenced is not necessarily second-
hand: I think it possible that a reader with a sensitive ear, a dispas-
sionate point of view, and a thorough knowledge of the poetry of
Hardy, say, would find as much difference as similarity between a
poem of mine, influenced by him, and one of Hardy's own.'

In one case, until I pointed this out, a scholar actually failed to
observe the initials under the titles of each pastiche in the *Florence:
Works of Art** section of *An Italian Visit*. Earlier I wrote of hero-
worship as a recurrent theme. I think it is one of the constituents of
these pastiches. There are certainly many examples of this in music.

Cecil matched the subjects of some of the Florentine pictures and sculpture he most loved, with poems in the style of poets he deeply admired: Yeats, Hardy, Robert Frost, W. H. Auden and Dylan Thomas. He wrote 'in the style of' and was admonished for being merely imitative . . .

At his best, he was a formidable craftsman. He was a storyteller in verse. This mastery of the narrative – a rare gift today – was shown first in *A Time to Dance*. Part of it is a gripping tale of a flight to Australia by two men in a decrepit aircraft after the First World War. Cecil had a tremendous reverence for brave men of action, and he had a passion for flying. The poem is an extraordinary feat of technique: long, rhythmic, 'airborne' lines, containing rhymes, half rhymes and internal rhymes (very much part of his 'voice'). He was to demonstrate this narrative skill again in 'The Nabara' (*Overtures to Death*).

'They preferred, because of the rudeness of their heart, to die rather than to surrender.'

Phase One

Freedom is more than a word, more than the base coinage
Of statesmen, the tyrant's dishonoured cheque, or the
                              dreamer's mad
Inflated currency. She is mortal, we know, and made
In the image of simple men who have no taste for carnage
But sooner kill and are killed than see that image
                              betrayed.
Mortal she is, yet rising always refreshed from her ashes:
She is bound to earth, yet she flies as high as a passage
                              bird
To home wherever man's heart with seasonal warmth is
                              stirred:
Innocent is her touch as the dawn's, but still it unleashes
The ravisher shades of envy. Freedom is more than a
                              word . . .

17

He was over forty when, after the war, he was able to afford his first holiday abroad and immediately he fell in love with Italy, like so many poets before him. Later, we did the journeys all over again together. 'Flight to Italy' was exactly as he told it in *An Italian Visit*. (It was before the days of jet aircraft, and I did not share his wild elation at take-off or when 'the atrocious Alps' were, literally, upon us, not below, and we eventually landed in Milan in a turmoil of forked lightning.) In the middle of the narrative is a contemplative passage I often quote to people who are recovering from illness and finding – as we all do – that convalescence can be the hardest part:

> . . . After a hard winter, on the first warm day
> The invalid venturing out into the rock-garden,
> Pale as a shaft of December sunshine, pauses,
> All at sea among the aubretia, the alyssum
> And arabis – halts and moves on how warily,
> As if to take soundings where the blossom foams and
> >   tumbles:
> But what he does sound is the depth of his own weakness
> At last, as never when pain-storms lashed him.
> So we, convalescent from routine's long fever,
> Plummeting our gaze down to river and plain,
> Question if indeed that dazzling world beneath us
> Be truth or delirium; and finding still so tentative
> The answer, can gauge how nearly we were ghosts,
> How far we must travel yet to flesh and blood . . .

In *Pegasus*, the narrative poems are new workings of Greek legends. The title poem is a powerful allegory about the creative process; a large number of his poems were about writing. The allegories 'A Failure'* and 'The Unwanted' (*Poems 1943–1947*), 'Final Instructions' (*Pegasus*) and 'Circus Lion' (*The Gate*) say a great deal about the discipline, devotion and pain of being a poet. In a lighter mood is a charming poem with an intricate, elegant stanza form dedicated to Robert Frost, called 'Sheepdog Trials in Hyde Park' (*The Gate*). Cecil challenged Frost to write one too, when, in 1957, they spent an afternoon together at this unlikely entertainment for a

18

New England farmer.

> . . . What's needfully done in the solitude of sheep-runs –
> Those tough, real tasks – becomes this stylized game,
> A demonstration of intuitive wit
> Kept natural by the saving grace of error.
> To lift, to fetch, to drive, to shed, to pen
> Are acts I recognize, with all they mean
> Of shepherding the unruly, for a kind of
> Controlled woolgathering is my work too.

At this time he wrote his first Dramatic Monologue for me: 'Ariadne on Naxos'*. He never succeeded in writing a play, but had a great gift for dialogue in poetry (and in the detective novels written by his alter ego Nicholas Blake). Later, in *The Gate*, he wrote two more Dramatic Monologues: 'The Disabused' (which he performed brilliantly and chillingly) and 'Not Proven'*, which he dedicated to our friend, George Rylands, the distinguished scholar, with whom we gave many recitals, and who was a co-founder of the Apollo Society.

In 1940 Cecil published his translation of Virgil's *Georgics*.* He had been a classical scholar at Wadham College, Oxford, and all his translations were exact, as well as being poems in their own right. He set out to steer the course between 'the twin vulgarities of flashy colloquialism and perfunctory grandiloquence'. He was a country-man for preference and was always minutely observant and accurate in his study of nature and the land. This is evident in all the poems. He felt intensely patriotic about his roots in the countryside on the Dorset/Devon border, and the threat of invasion intensified these feelings. Through them he was linked to Virgil, who had written of the land and husbandry with such tenderness all those centuries before.

In *Poems 1943–1947* there is his fine translation of Paul Valéry's *Le Cimetière marin* ('The Graveyard by the Sea'). It is faithful, and it is a poem of his own. I felt impelled to go there after his death, when the Spenders were giving me refuge in Provence. Natasha and I started out very early before the blistering heat of a July day. She drove me to Sète; we arrived at noon. It was extraordinary – we had walked into the poem (Cecil himself had never seen the graveyard).

> This quiet roof, where dove-sails saunter by,
> Between the pines, the tombs, throbs visibly.
> Impartial noon patterns the sea in flame –
> That sea for ever starting and re-starting.
> When thought has had its hour, oh how rewarding
> Are the long vistas of celestial calm!
>
> What grace of light, what pure toil goes to form
> The manifold diamond of the elusive foam!
> What peace I feel begotten at that source!
> When sunlight rests upon a profound sea,
> Time's air is sparkling, dream is certainty –
> Pure artifice both of an eternal Cause . . .

The last volume to be published in his lifetime was *The Whispering Roots*, in 1970, when his health had been failing for many years. More than half the poems spring from his Anglo-Irish provenance: the childhood memories; his Goldsmith ancestry; our 1966 visit to Dublin to commemorate the Easter Rising of 1916 (there were many other Dublin visits); the glorious summers we spent yearly with our children in Connemara and County Mayo – 'a source held near and dear'. In this book there are thirty-seven different stanza forms in thirty-four poems, and only one is repeated. Of a particular anonymous review of the poems Professor Samuel Hynes said, five years after C's death: 'It was not so much a review, I thought, as a literary mugging.' The reviewer, Geoffrey Grigson, had not had one good word to say about a single poem, and it was the last piece that Cecil ever read about his work before he died. It was a cruel blow to one who was always magnanimous, and had spent years of his life helping other writers. It was in character that he behaved stoically. I discovered we were each hiding the review from the other. We were not subscribers to the periodical, but 'well wishers' had posted it.

The *vers d'occasion* are verses with no pretension to being poetry, and they bring me back to his craftsmanship. First of all he made it clear on becoming Poet Laureate that he would try to involve himself in public issues that attracted him and needed support, not just Royal events. The variety of subjects speaks for itself, and I have no doubt that he would feel passionately about any number of the world's problems that concern us all today. As it was, I like to recollect his enchanting, challenging smile (grin, really) when he said to me: 'If I can write some verses on the amalgamation of six Teesside boroughs I shall feel I've really achieved something.' The many admirers of our friend Ronald Searle will look with affection (I hope) on 'A Short Dirge for St. Trinian's' written when the artist wished to bury the girls formally and finally.

When I edited *Posthumous Poems* I did not include, 'At Lemmons', the last poem he wrote on his deathbed (called by Professor Hynes 'a small masterpiece – reticent and calm, and very moving'). The reason for this is that it had already been included in a selection of *Poems 1925–1972*, many of them very much abridged without my fore-knowledge. If I had been consulted, I would not have given permission for the wildly random cuts. 'Either the whole poem or not at all,' I would have said. I wish I had re-published 'At Lemmons' at the end of *Posthumous Poems*. However, the last poem in that volume, 'Children Leaving Home', was his moving valedictory to Tamasin and Daniel. They must have thought he was detached, which is not uncommon with artists who are preoccupied. In his case it was also a conscious effort 'to ride them on a loose rein' (his phrase). He was an affectionate, reassuring and sage parent who had much to teach me, and here again 'the love is proved in the letting go'. All too soon they had to go forth. They were eighteen and just fifteen.

Cecil is buried in Stinsford churchyard, very near Thomas Hardy. Samuel Hynes said: 'His burial there seems to me entirely appropriate, not because he was of the stature of Hardy, who seems more and more clearly to be the greatest of modern English poets, but because he was of Hardy's company, a decent minor poet in the same tradition. By writing in the English lyric tradition, he helped to keep that tradition alive, and earned his place with Hardy in Stinsford churchyard.' I can picture again that special, gratified smile were he to read such a compliment, and happy incredulity at the knowledge that he was buried there in his beloved Dorset. 'The writing of poetry,' Cecil once wrote, 'is a vocation, a game, a habit, and a search for truth.' His life's work was all of these, and much more.

> . . . *Shall I be gone long?*
> For ever and a day.
> *To whom there belong?*
> Ask the stone to say,
> Ask my song . . .
> 'Is It Far to Go?' *Poems 1943–1947*

JILL BALCON

PREFACE*

The publisher has asked me to write a preface for this volume of my selected poems. About the choice of them there is little to be said, except that they had to be taken in fairly equal proportions from my earlier books, published by the Hogarth Press, and my more recent ones, published by Jonathan Cape. To what extent this selection is 'representative', or might enable a reader to 'trace the poet's development', I cannot say. Looking back over my verse of the last twenty years, to make the selection, I was struck, as I have been before, by its lack of development – in the sense of one poetic phase emerging recognizably from the previous one and leading inevitably to the next: it would be all much tidier and more in accordance with critical specifications, were this not so. But my verse seems to me a series of fresh beginnings, rather than a continuous line. Change I *can* see: change, but I hope not decay. My later work, as far as I may judge, presents a good deal more variety both in subject matter and in verse forms, a more sensuous appeal, and a greater flexibility of line, than my earlier. This is partly, no doubt, because my interests have changed and my sympathies perhaps widened. At the same time, it is only fair to inform the reader that, in the view of some critics, my verse has deteriorated since the early 'school of social consciousness' days into an anti-social or at any rate a-social preoccupation with the past and with traditional forms.

Change of character there certainly has been. Not that poems are often the *immediate* product of such changes. What happens, as far as I can make out, is that I have some deep violent experience which, like an earthquake, throws up layers of my past that were

---

* Written by Day Lewis for the 1951 *Selected Poems* (Penguin). The final section following the asterisks on page 27 was written in 1968 as a preface to the third edition (Penguin, 1969).

23

inaccessible to me poetically till then. During the last war, for instance, I found myself able to use in verse for the first time images out of my own childhood. The new material thrown up, the new contours which life presents as a result of the seismic experience, may demand a new kind of poem. It is here that change of technique appears. If the poet is, as Yeats became, an original poet, this change will be largely an affair between his imagination and his new material. If, like myself, he is a writer still much open to the influence of other poets, he will often find that he has more or less consciously used some other poet to mediate between his material and his imagination. I myself have been technically influenced, and enabled to clarify my thoughts, by such diverse poets as Yeats, Wordsworth, Robert Frost, Virgil, Valéry, W. H. Auden, and Hardy. They suggested to me ways of saying what I had to say. Any given poem thus influenced is not necessarily secondhand: I think it possible that a reader with a sensitive ear, a dispassionate point of view, and a thorough knowledge of the poetry of Hardy, say, would find as much difference as similarity between a poem of mine, influenced by him, and one of Hardy's own.

But that is by the way. What is important is that the reader should become aware both of the uniqueness of a poem and of its family resemblances. To realize its uniqueness – the quality that makes it different from any other poem – he must respond to it directly, spontaneously, positively. To approach a new poem, armed with all the latest instruments of criticism, and ask these to tell us whether we ought to admire or dislike it, is none the less an imbecility for being rather common practice today. We must be able to enjoy before we can learn to discriminate. The chief value of criticism, for the ordinary reader, is to deepen his understanding of a poem which already appeals to him, by indicating its family likenesses – its affinities in style, thought and experience, with other poems; its place in the tradition. But tradition is not a museum: it is a two-way traffic. The major poets, who enlarge the tradition, not only open the way for a new poetry; their own work is illuminated, reflected back on, by the work of lesser poets they influence. So we must never think of 'modern poetry' as something in a vacuum, or something that started in 1900, or 1917, or 1930. Every good poem has grown out of the

24

compost of all the poetry ever written, just as every original poet has been accused in his time, as poets are today, of obscurity, of breaking the rules and flouting the tradition. Modern poetry is every poem, whether written last year or five centuries ago, that has meaning for us still. In all ages there have been people nagging about the incompetence and unintelligibility of the verse of their contemporaries, and other people acclaiming it as the highest peak of poetic achievement, and yet other people to tell each poet exactly how he ought to be writing and conducting his life. These nuisances may do a certain amount of damage temporarily. But time sorts it all out. And in the meantime each poet must go on writing as best he may, learning from his own mistakes, learning to stop worrying about his stature, his rank in the hierarchy (for 'there is no competition') and to become ever more fully absorbed by the immediate task.

A poem, Robert Frost has said, 'begins in delight and ends in wisdom'. This is true, in a way, for the writer also. Poetry is a vocation, a habit, and a search for truth. We begin, young, with no equipment but a love for words and a special kind of temperament. We go on writing verse, if we do go on, because it has become a habit to play with words and to rely on them for the orientation of our interests. As we accumulate experience, we begin to perceive, sooner or later, that every poem is an attempt to compose our memories and to interpret this experience to our own satisfaction. We write in order to understand, not in order to be understood; though, the more successfully a poem has interpreted to its writer the meaning of his own experience, the more widely will it be 'understood' in the long run. The reader's progress is something similar. As a child he will have delighted in words and rhythms for their own sake. In adolescence, and perhaps for some years later, if he reads poetry at all, he is looking chiefly for a personal relevance: he wants the poem which will accord with his own kind of fantasies about life or support his fragmentary knowledge of it. It is only when we have done much and suffered much that we are able at all surely to distinguish the poetry in which sensuous and moral truth lie deepest; and by then, too often, our literary sympathies have hardened, so that we are prevented by its unfamiliar idiom from recognizing such truth in new poetry when we see it. Concerning poetic truth – that is, the re-ordering, re-creating and interpreting of human experience through poetry – both poet and reader have to make an act of faith. Each must believe that life holds certain kinds of truth which can best, or only, be conveyed through the medium of art, and that poetry has not been superseded in this function by any other art. It is a difficult faith today. Yet it is vindicated every time a poem, receiving the assent of heart and mind together, makes us feel, if only for an hour, at one with life and whole in ourselves.

It may be that such generalizations are out of place in a preface. I do not want the reader to think that absolute laws can be laid down for the writing or the reading of poetry. Perhaps I should, instead, have been taking him on a conducted tour of the poems he can find in my own books, pointing out their beauties and defects? I could show him where emotion, applied too raw, has eaten holes in the fabric of a poem, and where it has been more successfully deper-sonalized: where, through lack of patience, a poem has taken a wrong turning and ended up in a blind alley; or the very place where some apparently adventitious thing – the need for a certain rhyme or cadence – gave me a line which altered in the right direction a poem's whole course. I could point out how, during my so-called 'political' period, most of my poems were in fact about love or death: how, contrary to received opinion about modern verse, nearly all my poems 'rhyme and scan'; and how, contrary to the preconceived opinions of some, they are not always less experimental in nature when they are more traditional in idiom: how an over-enthusiastic, often perfunctory use of 'modern' imagery is gradually replaced by a more personal yet wider field of images: how certain characteris-tics keep cropping up throughout my work – hero-worship, fear, compassion, the divided mind, a prevailing sense of the transience of things: and how, whatever its apparent focus of the moment – pol-itics, the birth of a child, love for a woman, youthful memories, the apprehension or impact of war – however much its style is altered from time to time by the demands of some new experience or ruling passion, there runs through it all an unbroken thread, the search for personal identity, the poet's relentless compulsion to know himself.

But it is best that the reader should discover such points for himself. Many of them he would find equally applicable to any other living poet. Besides, the poet is not the best expositor of his own work; for, if there is one thing which surpasses his ardour of concentration in writing a poem, it is the extreme sense of detachment he feels when it has been written. This is not the kind of detachment which is proper in a critic: it is that of the maker who, knowing that 'every attempt is a wholly new start and a different kind of failure', must cut himself free from each failure in order to make the next attempt.

1951   C. Day Lewis

*   *   *

Any choice a poet makes from his own work is an arbitrary one. For *him*, the important thing is not what he has written but that he should go on writing. When Emily Dickinson said 'Art is a house which tries to be haunted', she said it all. We cannot explain, let alone command, the presence of that mysterious visitant who, perhaps only a few times in his life, enters a poet's work and transforms it from verse to poetry: this is the kind of grace which I tried to picture in 'Final Instructions'. All we can do is to build each house as competently as we can – and hope for the best.

We are concerned always with techniques of putting words together so that they *give* experience. Technique is much more than a servant: it defines experience by exploring it, and renders into art the raw material of reality.

I myself have always been challenged and captivated by problems of form. More and more I have come to realize that, for me at least, strict verse-forms are active discoverers of meaning. I believe they are liberating and felicitous, rather than constricting or deadening. I tried to put this in the second stanza of 'On Not Saying Everything' – a poem in praise of limitations, which I would leave as a last word.

1968   C. Day Lewis

from **TRANSITIONAL POEM**

MY LOVE IS A TOWER

My love is a tower.
Standing up in her
I parley with planets
And the casual wind.
Arcturus may grind
Against our wall: – he whets
A tropic appetite,
And decorates our night.
'What happier place
For Johnny Head-in-Air,
Who never would hear
Time mumbling at the base?'

I will not hear, for she's
My real Antipodes,
And our ingrowing loves
Shall meet below earth's spine
And there shall intertwine,
Though Babel falls above.
Time, we allow, destroys
All aërial toys:
But to assail love's heart
He has no strategy,
Unless he suck up the sea
And pull the earth apart.

HOW THEY WOULD JEER AT US

How they would jeer at us –
Ulysses, Herodotus,
The hard-headed Phœnicians
Or, of later nations,
Columbus, the Pilgrim Fathers
And a thousand others
Who laboured only to find
Some pittance of new ground,
Merchandise or women.
Those rude and bourgeois seamen
Got glory thrown in
As it were with every ton
Of wave that swept their boat,
And would have preferred a coat
For keeping off the spray.

Since the heroes lie
Entombed with the recipe
Of epic in their heart,
And have buried – it seems – that art
Of minding one's own business
Magnanimously, for us
There's nothing but to recant
Ambition, and be content
Like the poor child at play
To find a holiday
In the sticks and mud
Of a familiar road.

DESIRE IS A WITCH

Desire is a witch
And runs against the clock.
It can unstitch
The decent hem
Where space tacks on to time:
It can unlock
Pandora's privacies.

It puffs in these
Top-gallants of the mind,
And away I stand
On the elemental gale
Into an ocean
That the liar Lucian
Had never dared retail.

When my love leans with all
Her shining breast and shoulder,
I know she is older
Than Ararat the hill,
And yet more young
Than the first daffodil
That ever shews a spring.

When her eyes delay
On me, so deep are they
Tunnelled by love, although
You poured Atlantic
In this one and Pacific
In the other, I know
They would not overflow.

Desire clicks back
Like cuckoo into clock;
Leaves me to explain
Eyes that a tear will drown
And a body where youth
Nor age will long remain
To implicate the truth.

It seems that we must call
Anything truth whose well
Is deep enough;
For the essential
Philosopher-stone, desire,
Needs no other proof
Than its own fire.

WHEN NATURE PLAYS

When nature plays hedge-schoolmaster,
Shakes out the gaudy map of summer
And shows me charabanc, rose, barley-ear
And every bright-winged hummer,

He only would require of me
To be the sponge of natural laws
And learn no more of that cosmography
Than passes through the pores.

Why must I then unleash my brain
To sweat after some revelation
Behind the rose, heedless if truth maintain
On the rose-bloom her station?

When bullying April bruised mine eyes
With sleet-bound appetites and crude
Experiments of green, I still was wise
And kissed the blossoming rod.

Now summer brings what April took,
Riding with fanfares from the south,
And I should be no Solomon to look
My Sheba in the mouth.

Charabancs shout along the lane
And summer gales bay in the wood
No less superbly because I can't explain
What I have understood.

Let logic analyse the hive,
Wisdom's content to have the honey:
So I'll go bite the crust of things and thrive
While hedgerows still are sunny.

FOR I HAD BEEN A MODERN MOTH

For I had been a modern moth and hurled
Myself on many a flaming world,
To find its globe was glass.
In you alone
I met the naked light, by you became
Veteran of a flame
That burns away all but the warrior bone.
And I shall know, if time should falsify
This star the company of my night,
Mine is the heron's flight
Which makes a solitude of any sky.

WITH ME, MY LOVER MAKES

With me, my lover makes
   The clock assert its chime:
But when she goes, she takes
   The mainspring out of time.

Yet this time-wrecking charm
   Were better than love dead
And its hollow alarum
   Hammered out on lead.

Why should I fear that Time
   Will superannuate
These workmen of my rhyme –
   Love, despair and hate?

Fleeing the herd, I came
   To a graveyard on a hill,
And felt its mould proclaim
   The bone gregarious still.

Boredoms and agonies
   Work out the rhythm of bone: –
No peace till creature his
   Creator has outgrown.

Passion dies from the heart
   But to infect the marrow;
Holds dream and act apart
   Till the man discard his narrow

Sapience and folly
   Here, where the graves slumber
In a green melancholy
   Of overblown summer.

THOSE HIMALAYAS OF THE MIND

Those Himalayas of the mind
Are not so easily possessed:
There's more than precipice and storm
Between you and your Everest.

You who declare the peak of peaks
Alone will satisfy your want,
Can you distil a grain of snow?
Can you digest an adamant?

Better by far the household cock
Scratching the common yard for corn,
Whose rainy voice all night at will
Can signify a private dawn.

Another bird, sagacious too,
Circles in plain bewilderment
Where shoulder to shoulder long waves march
Towards a magnetic continent.

'What are these rocks impede our pomp?'
Gesticulating to the sun
The waves part ranks, sidle and fume,
Then close behind them and march on.

The waves advance, the Absolute Cliffs
Unaccountably repel:
They linger grovelling; where assault
Has failed, attrition may tell.

The bird sees nothing to the point;
Shrugs an indifferent wing; proceeds
From rock to rock in the mid-ocean
Peering for barnacles and weeds.

THE HAWK COMES DOWN FROM THE AIR

The hawk comes down from the air.
Sharpening his eye upon
A wheeling horizon
Turned scrutiny to prayer.

He guessed the prey that cowers
Below, and learnt to keep
The distance which can strip
Earth to its blank contours.

Then trod the air, content
With contemplation till
The truth of valley and hill
Should be self-evident.

Or as the little lark
Who veins the sky with song,
Asking from dawn to dark
No revenues of spring:

But with the night descends
Into his chosen tree,
And the famed singer ends
In anonymity.

So from a summer's height
I come into my peace;
The wings have earned their night,
And the song may cease.

from FROM FEATHERS TO IRON

SUPPOSE THAT WE

Suppose that we, tomorrow or the next day,
Came to an end – in storm the shafting broken,
Or a mistaken signal, the flange lifting –
Would that be premature, a text for sorrow?

Say what endurance gives or death denies us.
Love's proved in its creation, not eternity:
Like leaf or linnet the true heart's affection
Is born, dies later, asks no reassurance.

Over dark wood rises one dawn felicitous,
Bright through awakened shadows fall her crystal
Cadenzas, and once for all the wood is quickened.
So our joys visit us, and it suffices.

Nor fear we now to live who in the valley
Of the shadow of life have found a causeway;
For love restores the nerve and love is under
Our feet resilient. Shall we be weary?

Some say we walk out of Time altogether
This way into a region where the primrose
Shows an immortal dew, sun at meridian
Stands up for ever and in scent the lime tree.

This is a land which later we may tell of.
Here-now we know, what death cannot diminish
Needs no replenishing; yet certain are, though
Dying were well enough, to live is better.

Passion has grown full man by his first birthday.
Running across the bean-fields in a south wind,
Fording the river mouth to feel the tide-race –
Child's play that was, though proof of our possessions.

Now our research is done, measured the shadow,
The plains mapped out, the hills a natural boundary.
Such and such is our country. There remains to
Plough up the meadowland, reclaim the marshes.

BEAUTY'S END IS IN SIGHT

Beauty's end is in sight,
Terminus where all feather joys alight.
    Wings that flew lightly
    Fold and are iron. We see
The thin end of mortality.

We must a little part,
And sprouting seed crack our cemented heart.
    Who would get an heir
    Initial loss must bear:
A part of each will be elsewhere.

What life may now decide
Is past the clutch of caution, the range of pride.
    Speaking from the snow
    The crocus lets me know
That there is life to come, and go.

NOW SHE IS LIKE THE WHITE TREE-ROSE

Now she is like the white tree-rose
That takes a blessing from the sun:
Summer has filled her veins with light,
And her warm heart is washed with noon.

Or as a poplar, ceaselessly
Gives a soft answer to the wind:
Cool on the light her leaves lie sleeping,
Folding a column of sweet sound.

Powder the stars. Forbid the night
To wear those brilliants for a brooch
So soon, dark death, you may close down
The mines that made this beauty rich.

Her thoughts are pleiads, stooping low
O'er glades where nightingale has flown:
And like the luminous night around her
She has at heart a certain dawn.

REST FROM LOVING

Rest from loving and be living.
Fallen is fallen past retrieving
The unique flyer dawn's dove
Arrowing down feathered with fire.

Cease denying, begin knowing.
Comes peace this way here comes renewing
With dower of bird and bud knocks
Loud on winter wall on death's door.

Here's no meaning but of morning.
Naught soon of night but stars remaining,
Sink lower, fade, as dark womb
Recedes creation will step clear.

Waning is now the sensual eye
Allowed no flaw upon the skin
And burnt away wrinkle and feature,
Fed with pure spirit from within.

Nesciently that vision works.
Just so the pure night-eye, the moon,
Labours, a monumental mason,
To gloss over a world of stone.

Look how she marbled heath and terrace,
Effacing boundary and date.
She took the sky; earth was below her
A shining shell, a featherweight.

No more may pupil love bend over
A plane theorem, black and white.
The interlocking hours revolve,
The globe goes lumbering into light.

Admiral earth breaks out his colours
Bright at the forepeak of the day;
Hills in their hosts escort the sun
And valleys welcome him their way.

Shadow takes depth and shape turns solid:
Far-ranging, the creative eye
Sees arable, marsh, enclosed and common,
Assents to multiplicity.

AS ONE WHO WANDERS

As one who wanders into old workings
Dazed by the noonday, desiring coolness,
Has found retreat barred by fall of rockface;
Gropes through galleries where granite bruises
Taut palm and panic patters close at heel;
Must move forward as tide to the moon's nod,
As mouth to breast in blindness is beckoned.
Nightmare nags at his elbow and narrows
Horizon to pinpoint, hope to hand's breadth.
Slow drip the seconds, time is stalactite,
For nothing intrudes here to tell the time,
Sun marches not, nor moon with muffled step.
He wants an opening, – only to break out,
To see the dark glass cut by day's diamond,
To relax again in the lap of light.

But we seek a new world through old workings,
Whose hope lies like seed in the loins of earth,
Whose dawn draws gold from the roots of darkness.
Not shy of light nor shrinking from shadow
Like Jesuits in jungle we journey
Deliberately bearing to brutish tribes
Christ's assurance, arts of agriculture.
As a train that travels underground track
Feels current flashed from far-off dynamos,
Our wheels whirling with impetus elsewhere
Generated we run, are ruled by rails.
Train shall spring from tunnel to terminus,
Out on to plain shall the pioneer plunge,
Earth reveal what veins fed, what hill covered.
Lovely the leap, explosion into light.

NOW THE FULL-THROATED DAFFODILS

Now the full-throated daffodils,
Our trumpeters in gold,
Call resurrection from the ground
And bid the year be bold.

Today the almond tree turns pink,
The first flush of the spring;
Winds loll and gossip through the town
Her secret whispering.

Now too the bird must try his voice
Upon the morning air;
Down drowsy avenues he cries
A novel great affair.

He tells of royalty to be;
How with her train of rose
Summer to coronation comes
Through waving wild hedgerows.

Today crowds quicken in a street,
The fish leaps in the flood:
Look there, gasometer rises,
And here bough swells to bud.

For our love's luck, our stowaway,
Stretches in his cabin;
Our youngster joy barely conceived
Shows up beneath the skin.

Our joy was but a gusty thing
Without sinew or wit,
An infant flyaway; but now
We make a man of it.

DO NOT EXPECT AGAIN A PHŒNIX HOUR

Do not expect again a phœnix hour,
The triple-towered sky, the dove complaining,
Sudden the rain of gold and heart's first ease
Tranced under trees by the eldritch light of sundown.

By a blazed trail our joy will be returning:
One burning hour throws light a thousand ways,
And hot blood stays into familiar gestures.
The best years wait, the body's plenitude.

Consider then, my lover, this is the end
Of the lark's ascending, the hawk's unearthly hover:
Spring season is over soon and first heatwave;
Grave-browed with cloud ponders the huge horizon.

Draw up the dew. Swell with pacific violence.
Take shape in silence. Grow as the clouds grew.
Beautiful brood the cornlands, and you are heavy;
Leafy the boughs – they also hide big fruit.

BEAUTY BREAKS GROUND

Beauty breaks ground, oh, in strange places.
Seen after cloudburst down the bone-dry watercourses,
In Texas a great gusher, a grain-
Elevator in the Ukraine plain;
To a new generation turns new faces.

Here too fountains will soon be flowing.
Empty the hills where love was lying late, was playing,
Shall spring to life: we shall find there
Milk and honey for love's heir,
Shadow from sun also, deep ground for growing.

My love is a good land. The stranger
Entering here was sure he need prospect no further.
Acres that were the eyes' delight
Now feed another appetite.
What formed her first for seed, for crop must change her.

This is my land, I've overheard it
Making a promise out of clay. All is recorded –
Early green, drought, ripeness, rainfall,
Our village fears and festivals,
When the first tractor came and how we cheered it.

And as the wind whose note will deepen
In the upgrowing tree, who runs for miles to open
His throat above the wood, my song
With that increasing life grew strong,
And will have there a finished form to sleep in.

from THE MAGNETIC MOUNTAIN

NOW TO BE WITH YOU

Now to be with you, elate, unshared,
My kestrel joy, O hoverer in wind,
Over the quarry furiously at rest
Chaired on shoulders of shouting wind.

Where's that unique one, wind and wing married,
Aloft in contact of earth and ether;
Feathery my comet, Oh too often
From heaven harried by carrion cares.

No searcher may hope to flush that fleet one
Not to be found by gun or glass,
In old habits, last year's hunting-ground,
Whose beat is wind-wide, whose perch a split second.

But surely will meet him, late or soon,
Who turns a corner into new territory;
Spirit mating afresh shall discern him
On the world's noon-top purely poised.

Void are the valleys, in town no trace,
And dumb the sky-dividing hills:
Swift outrider of lumbering earth
Oh hasten hither my kestrel joy!

BUT TWO THERE ARE

But Two there are, shadow us everywhere
And will not let us be till we are dead,
Hardening the bones, keeping the spirit spare,
Original in water, earth and air,
Our bitter cordial, our daily bread.

Turning over old follies in ante-room,
For first-born waiting or for late reprieve,
Watching the safety-valve, the slackening loom,
Abed, abroad, at every turn and tomb
A shadow starts, a hand is on your sleeve.

O you, my comrade, now or tomorrow flayed
Alive, crazed by the nibbling nerve; my friend
Whom hate has cornered or whom love betrayed,
By hunger sapped, trapped by a stealthy tide,
Brave for so long but whimpering in the end:

Such are the temporal princes, fear and pain,
Whose borders march with the ice-fields of death,
And from that servitude escape there's none
Till in the grave we set up house alone
And buy our liberty with our last breath.

LET US BE OFF!

Let us be off! Our steam
Is deafening the dome.
The needle in the gauge
Points to a long-banked rage,
And trembles there to show
What a pressure's below.
Valve cannot vent the strain
Nor iron ribs refrain
That furnace in the heart.
Come on, make haste and start
Coupling-rod and wheel
Welded of patient steel,
Piston that will not stir
Beyond the cylinder
To take in its stride
A teeming countryside.

A countryside that gleams
In the sun's weeping beams;
Where wind-pump, byre and barrow
Are mellowed to mild sorrow,
Agony and sweat
Grown over with regret.
What golden vesper hours
Halo the old grey towers,
What honeyed bells in valleys
Embalm our faiths and follies!
Here are young daffodils
Wind-wanton, and the hills
Have made their peace with heaven.
Oh lovely the heart's haven,
Meadows of endless May,
A spirit's holiday!

Traveller, take care,
Pick no flowers there!

NEARING AGAIN THE LEGENDARY ISLE

Nearing again the legendary isle
Where sirens sang and mariners were skinned,
We wonder now what was there to beguile
That such stout fellows left their bones behind.

Those chorus-girls are surely past their prime,
Voices grow shrill and paint is wearing thin,
Lips that sealed up the sense from gnawing time
Now beg the favour with a graveyard grin.

We have no flesh to spare and they can't bite,
Hunger and sweat have stripped us to the bone;
A skeleton crew we toil upon the tide
And mock the theme-song meant to lure us on:

53

No need to stop the ears, avert the eyes
From purple rhetoric of evening skies.

LIVE YOU BY LOVE CONFINED

Live you by love confined,
There is no nearer nearness;
Break not his light bounds,
The stars' and seas' harness:
There is nothing beyond,
We have found the land's end.
We'll take no mortal wound
Who felt him in the furnace,
Drowned in his fierceness,
By his midsummer browned:
Nor ever lose awareness
Of nearness and farness
Who've stood at earth's heart careless
Of suns and storms around,
Who have leant on the hedge of the wind,
On the last ledge of darkness.

We are where love has come
To live: he is that river
Which flows and is the same;
He is not the famous deceiver
Nor early-flowering dream.
Content you. Be at home
In me. There's but one room
Of all the house you may never
Share, deny or enter.
There, as a candle's beam
Stands firm and will not waver
Spire-straight in a close chamber,

As though in shadowy cave a
Stalagmite of flame,
The integral spirit climbs
The dark in light for ever.

GOD IS A PROPOSITION

God is a proposition,
And we that prove him are his priests, his chosen.
From bare hypothesis
Of strata and wind, of stars and tides, watch me
Construct his universe,
A working model of my majestic notions,
A sum done in the head.
Last week I measured the light, his little finger;
The rest is a matter of time.

God is an electrician,
And they that worship him must worship him
In ampere and in volt.
Scrap sun and moon, your twilight of false gods:
X. is not here or there;
Whose lightning scrawls brief cryptograms on sky,
Easy for us to solve;
Whose motions fit our formulae, whose temple
Is a pure apparatus.

God is a statistician:
Offer him all the data; tell him your dreams.
What is your lucky number?
How do you react to bombs? Have you a rival?
Do you really love your wife?
Get yourself taped. Put soul upon the table:
Switch on the arc-lights; watch
Heart's beat, the secret agents of the blood.
Let every cell be observed.

God is a Good Physician,
Gives fruit for hygiene, crops for calories.
Don't touch that dirty man,
Don't drink from the same cup, sleep in one bed:
You know He would not like it.
Young men, cut out those visions, they're bad for the eyes:
I'll show you face to face
Eugenics, Eupeptics and Euthanasia,
The clinic Trinity.

TEMPT ME NO MORE

Tempt me no more; for I
Have known the lightning's hour,
The poet's inward pride,
The certainty of power.

Bayonets are closing round.
I shrink; yet I must wring
A living from despair
And out of steel a song.

Though song, though breath be short,
I'll share not the disgrace
Of those that ran away
Or never left the base.

Comrades, my tongue can speak
No comfortable words,
Calls to a forlorn hope,
Gives work and not rewards.

Oh keep the sickle sharp
And follow still the plough:
Others may reap, though some
See not the winter through.

Father, who endest all,
Pity our broken sleep;
For we lie down with tears
And waken but to weep.

And if our blood alone
Will melt this iron earth,
Take it. It is well spent
Easing a saviour's birth.

THOUGH WINTER'S BARRICADE DELAYS

Though winter's barricade delays,
Another season's in the air;
We'll sow the spring in our young days,
Found a Virginia everywhere.

Look where the ranks of crocuses
Their rebel colours will display
Coming with quick fire to redress
The balance of a wintry day.

Those daffodils that from the mould
Drawing a sweet breath soon shall flower,
With a year's labour get their gold
To spend it on a sunny hour.

They from earth's centre take their time
And from the sun what love they need:
The proud flower burns away its prime,
Eternity lies in the seed.

Follow the kestrel, south or north,
Strict eye, spontaneous wing can tell
A secret. Where he comes to earth
Is the heart's treasure. Mark it well.

Here he hovers. You're on the scent;
Magnetic mountain is not far,
Across no gulf or continent,
Not where you think but where you are.

Stake out your claim. Go downwards. Bore
Through the tough crust. Oh learn to feel
A way in darkness to good ore.
You are the magnet and the steel.

Out of that dark a new world flowers.
There in the womb, in the rich veins
Are tools, dynamos, bridges, towers,
Your tractors and your travelling-cranes.

YOU THAT LOVE ENGLAND

You that love England, who have an ear for her music,
The slow movement of clouds in benediction,
Clear arias of light thrilling over her uplands,
Over the chords of summer sustained peacefully;
Ceaseless the leaves' counterpoint in a west wind lively,
Blossom and river rippling loveliest allegro,
And the storms of wood strings brass at year's finale:
Listen. Can you not hear the entrance of a new theme?

You who go out alone, on tandem or on pillion,
Down arterial roads riding in April,
Or sad beside lakes where hill-slopes are reflected
Making fires of leaves, your high hopes fallen:
Cyclists and hikers in company, day excursionists,
Refugees from cursed towns and devastated areas;
Know you seek a new world, a saviour to establish
Long-lost kinship and restore the blood's fulfilment.

You who like peace, good sorts, happy in a small way
Watching birds or playing cricket with schoolboys,
Who pay for drinks all round, whom disaster chose not;
Yet passing derelict mills and barns roof-rent
Where despair has burnt itself out – hearts at a standstill,
Who suffer loss, aware of lowered vitality;
We can tell you a secret, offer a tonic; only
Submit to the visiting angel, the strange new healer.

You above all who have come to the far end, victims
Of a run-down machine, who can bear it no longer;
Whether in easy chairs chafing at impotence
Or against hunger, bullies and spies preserving
The nerve for action, the spark of indignation –
Need fight in the dark no more, you know your enemies.
You shall be leaders when zero hour is signalled,
Wielders of power and welders of a new world.

IN THESE OUR WINTER DAYS

In these our winter days
Death's iron tongue is glib
Numbing with fear all flesh upon
A fiery-hearted globe.

An age once green is buried,
Numbered the hours of light;
Blood-red across the snow our sun
Still trails his faint retreat.

Spring through death's iron guard
Her million blades shall thrust;
Love that was sleeping, not extinct,
Throw off the nightmare crust.

Eyes, though not ours, shall see
Sky-high a signal flame,
The sun returned to power above
A world, but not the same.

from A TIME TO DANCE

LEARNING TO TALK

See this small one, tiptoe on
The green foothills of the years,
Views a younger world than yours;
When you go down, he'll be the tall one.

Dawn's dew is on his tongue –
No word for what's behind the sky,
Naming all that meets the eye,
Pleased with sunlight over a lawn.

Hear his laughter. He can't contain
The exquisite moment overflowing.
Limbs leaping, woodpecker flying
Are for him and not hereafter.

Tongue trips, recovers, triumphs,
Turning all ways to express
What the forward eye can guess –
That time is his and earth young.

We are growing too like trees
To give the rising wind a voice:
Eagles shall build upon our verse,
Our winged seeds are tomorrow's sowing.

Yes, we learn to speak for all
Whose hearts here are not at home,
All who march to a better time
And breed the world for which they burn.

Though we fall once, though we often,
Though we fall to rise not again,
From our horizon sons begin;
When we go down, they will be tall ones.

THE CONFLICT

I sang as one
Who on a tilting deck sings
To keep men's courage up, though the wave hangs
That shall cut off their sun.

As storm-cocks sing,
Flinging their natural answer in the wind's teeth,
And care not if it is waste of breath
Or birth-carol of spring.

As ocean-flyer clings
To height, to the last drop of spirit driving on
While yet ahead is land to be won
And work for wings.

Singing I was at peace,
Above the clouds, outside the ring:
For sorrow finds a swift release in song
And pride its poise.

Yet living here,
As one between two massing powers I live
Whom neutrality cannot save
Nor occupation cheer.

None such shall be left alive:
The innocent wing is soon shot down,
And private stars fade in the blood-red dawn
Where two worlds strive.

The red advance of life
Contracts pride, calls out the common blood,
Beats song into a single blade,
Makes a depth-charge of grief.

Move then with new desires,
For where we used to build and love
Is no man's land, and only ghosts can live
Between two fires.

IN ME TWO WORLDS

In me two worlds at war
Trample the patient flesh,
This lighted ring of sense where clinch
Heir and ancestor.

This moving point of dust
Where past and future meet
Traces their battle-line and shows
Each thrust and counterthrust.

The armies of the dead
Are trenched within my bones,
My blood's their semaphore, their wings
Are watchers overhead.

Their captains stand at ease
As on familiar ground,
The veteran longings of the heart
Serve them for mercenaries.

Conscious of power and pride
Imperially they move
To pacify an unsettled zone –
The life for which they died.

But see, from vision's height
March down the men to come,
And in my body rebel cells
Look forward to the fight.

The insolence of the dead
Breaks on their solid front:
They tap my nerves for power, my veins
To stain their banners red.

These have the spirit's range,
The measure of the mind:
Out of the dawn their fire comes fast
To conquer and to change.

So heir and ancestor
Pursue the inveterate feud,
Making my senses' darkened fields
A theatre of war.

THE ECSTATIC

Lark, skylark, spilling your rubbed and round
Pebbles of sound in air's still lake,
Whose widening circles fill the noon; yet none
Is known so small beside the sun:

Be strong your fervent soaring, your skyward air!
Tremble there, a nerve of song!
Float up there where voice and wing are one,
A singing star, a note of light!

Buoyed, embayed in heaven's noon-wide reaches –
For soon light's tide will turn – Oh stay!
Cease not till day streams to the west, then down
That estuary drop down to peace.

TWO SONGS

I've heard them lilting at loom and belting,
Lasses lilting before dawn of day:
But now they are silent, not gamesome and gallant –
The flowers of the town are rotting away.

There was laughter and loving in the lanes at evening;
Handsome were the boys then, and girls were gay.
But lost in Flanders by medalled commanders
The lads of the village are vanished away.

Cursed be the promise that takes our men from us –
All will be champion if you choose to obey:
They fight against hunger but still it is stronger –
The prime of our land grows cold as the clay.

The women are weary, once lilted so merry,
Waiting to marry for a year and a day:
From wooing and winning, from owning or earning
The flowers of the town are all turned away.

Come, live with me and be my love,
And we will all the pleasures prove
Of peace and plenty, bed and board,
That chance employment may afford.

I'll handle dainties on the docks
And thou shalt read of summer frocks:
At evening by the sour canals
We'll hope to hear some madrigals.

Care on thy maiden brow shall put
A wreath of wrinkles, and thy foot
Be shod with pain: not silken dress
But toil shall tire thy loveliness.

Hunger shall make thy modest zone
And cheat fond death of all but bone –
If these delights thy mind may move,
Then live with me and be my love.

from A TIME TO DANCE

For those who had the power
    of the forest fires that burn
Leaving their source in ashes
    to flush the sky with fire:
Those whom a famous urn
    could not contain, whose passion
Brimmed over the deep grave
    and dazzled epitaphs:
For all that have won us wings
    to clear the tops of grief,
My friend who within me laughs
    bids you dance and sing.

Some set out to explore
    earth's limit, and little they recked if
Never their feet came near it
    outgrowing the need for glory:
Some aimed at a small objective
    but the fierce updraught of their spirit
Forced them to the stars.
    Are honoured in public who built
The dam that tamed a river;
    or holding the salient for hours
Against odds, cut off and killed,
    are remembered by one survivor.

All these. But most for those
    whom accident made great,
As a radiant chance encounter
    of cloud and sunlight grows
Immortal on the heart:
    whose gift was the sudden bounty
Of a passing moment, enriches
    the fulfilled eye for ever.
Their spirits float serene
    above time's roughest reaches,
But their seed is in us and over
    our lives they are evergreen.

from OVERTURES TO DEATH

SEX-CRIME

For one, the sudden fantastic grimace
Above, the red clown's-grin ripping the chalk sad sky,
Hailstones hatched out of midsummer, a face
Blanched with love's vile reversal.

                              The spirit died
First – such blank amazement took away its breath,
And let the body cry
Through the short scuffle and infamy of death.
For the other, who knows what nice proportion of loathing
And lust conjured the deep devil, created
That chance of incandescence? Figures here prove nothing.
One step took him through the roaring waterfall
That closed like a bead-curtain, left him alone with the writhing
Of what he loved or hated.
His hands leapt out: they took vengeance for all
Denials and soft answers. There was one who said
Long since, 'rough play will end in tears'. There was Cain
In the picture-book. Forgotten. Here is one dead,
And one could never be whole again.

                              The news
Broke a Sunday inertia: ring after ring
Across that smug mirror went echoing
And fainting out to the dim margins of incredulity.
A few raw souls accuse
Themselves of this felony and find not guilty –
Acquitted on a mere alibi or technical point.
Most see it as an island eruption, viewed
From the safe continent; not dreaming the same fire pent
Within their clay that warps
The night with fluent alarm, their own wrath spewed

Through the red craters of that undistinguished corpse.
All that has reached them is the seismic thrill:
The ornaments vibrate on the shelf; then they are still.
Snugly we settle down
Into our velvet and legitimate bed,
While news-sheets are yet falling all over the town
Like a white ash. Falling on one dead
And one can never be whole again.

                           You watch him
Pulpited in the dock, preaching repentance
While the two professionals in fancy dress
Manœuvre formally to score off him or catch him.
But grief has her conventions –
The opaque mask of misery will confess
Nothing, nor plead moving extenuations.
But you who crowd the court-room, will you never be called
To witness for the defence?

                             Accomplices,
All of you, now – though now is still too late –
Bring on the missing evidence! Reveal the coiled
Venom, the curse that needs
Only a touch to be articulate.
You, Judge, strip off! Show us the abscess boiling
Beneath your scarlet. Oh point, someone, to where it spreads
On every hand – the red, collusive stain . . .
All too well you have done your work: for one is dead,
And the other will not be whole again.

THE NABARA*

'They preferred, because of the rudeness of their heart,
to die rather than to surrender.'†

PHASE ONE

Freedom is more than a word, more than the base coinage
Of statesmen, the tyrant's dishonoured cheque, or the
                                        dreamer's mad
Inflated currency. She is mortal, we know, and made
In the image of simple men who have no taste for carnage
But sooner kill and are killed than see that image betrayed.
Mortal she is, yet rising always refreshed from her ashes:
She is bound to earth, yet she flies as high as a passage bird
To home wherever man's heart with seasonal warmth is stirred:
Innocent is her touch as the dawn's, but still it unleashes
The ravisher shades of envy. Freedom is more than a word.

I see man's heart two-edged, keen both for death and creation.
As a sculptor rejoices, stabbing and mutilating the stone
Into a shapelier life, and the two joys make one –
So man is wrought in his hour of agony and elation
To efface the flesh to reveal the crying need of his bone.
Burning the issue was beyond their mild forecasting
For those I tell of – men used to the tolerable joy and hurt
Of simple lives: they coveted never an epic part;
But history's hand was upon them and hewed an everlasting
Image of freedom out of their rude and stubborn heart.

The year, Nineteen-thirty-seven: month, March: the men,
                                        descendants
Of those Iberian fathers, the inquiring ones who would go
Wherever the sea-ways led: a pacific people, slow

---

* The episode upon which this poem is based is related in G. L. Steer's book *The Tree
of Gernika* about the Spanish Civil War.
† In italics are the words of Walsingham after the sea-battle between English and
Basques in 1350.

To feel ambition, loving their laws and their independence –
Men of the Basque country, the Mar Cantabrico.
Fishermen, with no guile outside their craft, they had weathered
Often the sierra-ranked Biscayan surges, the wet
Fog of the Newfoundland Banks: they were fond of *pelota*: they met
No game beyond their skill as they swept the sea together,
Until the morning they found the leviathan in their net.

Government trawlers *Nabara, Guipuzkoa, Bizkaya,*
Donostia, escorting across blockaded seas
Galdames with her cargo of nickel and refugees
From Bayonne to Bilbao, while the crest of war curled higher
Inland over the glacial valleys, the ancient ease.
On the morning of March the fifth, a chill North-Wester
                         fanned them,
Fogging the glassy waves: what uncharted doom lay low
There in the fog athwart their course, they could not know:
Stout were the armed trawlers, redoubtable those who
                         manned them –
Men of the Basque country, the Mar Cantabrico.

Slowly they nosed ahead, while under the chill North-Wester
Nervous the sea crawled and twitched like the skin of a beast
That dreams of the chase, the kill, the blood-beslavered feast:
They too, the light-hearted sailors, dreamed of a fine fiesta,
Flags and their children waving, when they won home from the east.
Vague as images seen in a misted glass or the vision
Of crystal-gazer, the ships huddled, receded, neared,
Threading the weird fog-maze that coiled their funnels and bleared
Day's eye. They were glad of the fog till *Galdames* lost position
– Their convoy, precious in life and metal – and disappeared.

But still they held their course, the confident ear-ringed captains,
Unerring towards the landfall, nor guessed how the land lay,
How the guardian fog was a guide to lead them all astray.
For now, at a wink, the mist rolled up like the film that curtains
A saurian's eye; and into the glare of an evil day

76

Bizkaya, Guipuzkoa, Nabara, and the little
Donostia stepped at intervals; and sighted, alas,
Blocking the sea and sky a mountain they might not pass,
An isle thrown up volcanic and smoking, a giant in metal
Astride their path – the rebel cruiser, *Canarias*.

A ship of ten thousand tons she was, a heavyweight fighter
To the cocky bantam trawlers: and under her armament
Of eight- and four-inch guns there followed obedient
Towards Pasajes a prize just seized, an Estonian freighter
Laden with arms the exporters of death to Spain had sent.
A hush, the first qualm of conflict, falls on the cruiser's burnished
Turrets, the trawlers' grimy decks: fiercer the lime-
Light falls, and out of the solemn ring the late mists climb,
And ship to ship the antagonists gaze at each other astonished
Across the quaking gulf of the sea for a moment's time.

The trawlers' men had no chance or wish to elude the fated
Encounter. Freedom to these was natural pride that runs
Hot as the blood, their climate and heritage, dearer than sons.
Bizkaya, Guipuzkoa, knowing themselves outweighted,
Drew closer to draw first blood with their pairs of four-inch guns.
Aboard *Canarias* the German gun-layers stationed
Brisk at their intricate batteries – guns and men both trained
To a hair in accuracy, aimed at a pitiless end –
Fired, and the smoke rolled forth over the unimpassioned
Face of a day where nothing certain but death remained.

PHASE TWO

The sound of the first salvo skimmed the ocean and thumped
Cape Machichaco's granite ribs: it rebounded where
The salt-sprayed trees grow tough from wrestling the wind:
                                        it jumped
From isle to rocky isle: it was heard by women while
They walked to shrine or market, a warning they must fear.

But, beyond their alarm, as
Though that sound were also a signal for fate to strip
Luck's last green shoot from the falling stock of the
                    Basques, *Galdames*
Emerged out of the mist that lingered to the west
Under the reeking muzzles of the rebel battleship:

Which instantly threw five shells over her funnel, and threw
Her hundred women and children into a slaughter-yard panic
On the deck they imagined smoking with worse than the foggy dew,
So that *Galdames* rolled as they slipped, clawed, trampled, reeled
Away from the gape of the cruiser's guns. A spasm galvanic,
Fear's chemistry, shocked the women's bodies, a moment before
Huddled like sheep in a mist, inert as bales of rag,
A mere deck-cargo; but more
Than furies now, for they stormed *Galdames'* bridge and swarmed
Over her captain and forced him to run up the white flag.

Signalling the Estonian, 'Heave-to', *Canarias* steamed
Leisurely over to make sure of this other prize:
Over-leisurely was her reckoning – she never dreamed
The Estonian in that pause could be snatched from her
                    shark-shape jaws
By ships of minnow size.
Meanwhile *Nabara* and *Guipuzkoa*, not reluctant
For closer grips while their guns and crews were still entire,
Thrust forward: twice *Guipuzkoa* with a deadly jolt was rocked, and
The sea spat up in geysers of boiling foam, as the cruiser's
Heavier guns boxed them in a torrid zone of fire.

And now the little *Donostia* who lay with her 75's
Dumb in the offing – her weapons against that leviathan
Impotent as pen-knives –
Witnessed a bold manœuvre, a move of genius, never
In naval history told. She saw *Bizkaya* run
Ahead of her consorts, a berserk atom of steel, audacious,
Her signal-flags soon to flutter like banderillas, straight

Towards the Estonian speeding, a young bull over the spacious
And foam-distraught arena, till the sides of the freight-ship
                                        screen her
From *Canarias* that will see the point of her charge too late.

'Who are you and where are you going?' the flags of
                        Bizkaya questioned.
'Carrying arms and forced to go to Pasajes,' replied
The Estonian. 'Follow me to harbour.' 'Cannot, am threatened.'
Bizkaya's last word – 'Turn at once!' – and she points her
                        peremptory guns
Against the freighter's mountainous flanks that blankly hide
This fluttering language and flaunt of signal insolence
From the eyes of *Canarias*. At last the rebels can see
That the two ships' talk meant a practical joke at their expense:
They see the Estonian veering away, to Bermeo steering,
Bizkaya under her lee.

(To the Basques that ship was a tonic, for she carried some
                        million rounds
Of ammunition: to hearts grown sick with hope deferred
And the drain of their country's wounds
She brought what most they needed in face of the aid evaded
And the cold delay of those to whom freedom was only a word.)*
Owlish upon the water sat the *Canarias*
Mobbed by those darting trawlers, and her signals blinked in vain
After the freighter, that still she believed too large to pass
Into Bermeo's port – a prize she fondly thought,
When she'd blown the trawlers out of the water, she'd take again.

---

* Cf. Byron's comments upon 'Non-Intervention' in *The Age of Bronze*:
>   Lone, lost, abandoned in their utmost need
>   By Christians, unto whom they gave their creed.
>   The desolated lands, the ravaged isle,
>   The fostered feud encouraged to beguile,
>   The aid evaded, and the cold delay
>   Prolonged but in the hope to make a prey: –
>   These, these shall tell the tale, and Greece can show
>   The false friend worse than the infuriate foe.

Brisk at their intricate batteries the German gun-layers go
About death's business, knowing their longer reach must foil
The impetus, break the heart of the government ships: each blow
Deliberately they aim, and tiger-striped with flame
Is the jungle mirk of the smoke as their guns leap and recoil.
The Newfoundland trawlers feel
A hail and hurricane the like they have never known
In all their deep-sea life: they wince at the squalls of steel
That burst on their open decks, rake them and leave them wrecks,
But still they fight on long into the sunless afternoon.

– Fought on, four guns against the best of the rebel navy,
Until *Guipuzkoa*'s crew could stanch the fires no more
That gushed from her gashes and seeped nearer the
                              magazine. Heavy
At heart they turned away for the Nervion that day:
Their ship, *Guipuzkoa*, wore
Flame's rose on her heart like a decoration of highest honour
As listing she reeled into Las Arenas; and in a row
On her deck there lay, smoke-palled, the oriflamme's
                              crackling banner
Above them, her dead – a quarter of the fishermen who had
                              fought her –
Men of the Basque country, the Mar Cantabrico.

PHASE THREE

And now the gallant *Nabara* was left in the ring alone,
The sky hollow around her, the fawning sea at her side:
But the ear-ringed crew in their berets stood to the guns, and cried
A fresh defiance down
The ebb of the afternoon, the battle's darkening tide.
Honour was satisfied long since; they had held and harried
A ship ten times their size; they well could have called it a day.
But they hoped, if a little longer they kept the cruiser in play,
Galdames with the wealth of life and metal she carried
Might make her getaway.

Canarias, though easily she outpaced and out-gunned her,
Finding this midge could sting
Edged off, and beneath a wedge of smoke steamed in a ring
On the rim of the trawler's range, a circular storm of thunder.
But always *Nabara* turned her broadside, manœuvring
To keep both guns on the target, scorning safety devices.
Slower now battle's tempo, irregular the beat
Of gunfire in the heart

Of the afternoon, the distempered sky sank to the crisis,
Shell-shocked the sea tossed and hissed in delirious heat.
The battle's tempo slowed, for the cruiser could take her time,
And the guns of *Nabara* grew
Red-hot, and of fifty-two Basque seamen had been her crew
Many were dead already, the rest filthy with grime
And their comrades' blood, weary with wounds all but a few.
Between two fires they fought, for the sparks that flashing spoke
From the cruiser's thunder-bulk were answered on their own craft
By traitor flames that crawled out of every cranny and rift
Blinding them all with smoke.
At half-past four *Nabara* was burning fore and aft.

What buoyancy of will
Was theirs to keep her afloat, no vessel now but a sieve –
So jarred and scarred, the rivets starting, no inch of her safe
From the guns of the foe that wrapped her in a cyclone of
                                        shrieking steel!
Southward the sheltering havens showed clear, the cliffs
                                        and the surf
Familiar to them from childhood, the shapes of a life still dear:
But dearer still to see
Those shores insured for life from the shadow of tyranny.
Freedom was not on their lips; it was what made them endure,
A steel spring in the yielding flesh, a thirst to be free.

And now from the little *Donostia* that lay with her 75's
Dumb in the offing, they saw *Nabara* painfully lower
A boat, which crawled like a shattered crab slower and slower
Towards them. They cheered the survivors, thankful to
                                        save these lives
At least. They saw each rower,
As the boat dragged alongside, was wounded – the oars they held
Dripping with blood, a bloody skein reeled out in their wake:
And they swarmed down the rope-ladders to rescue these
                                        men so weak
From wounds they must be hauled
Aboard like babies. And then they saw they had made a mistake.

For, standing up in the boat,
A man of that grimy boat's-crew hailed them: 'Our officer asks
You give us your bandages and all your water-casks,
Then run for Bermeo. We're going to finish this game of *pelota*.'
Donostia's captain begged them with tears to escape: but
                                        the Basques
Would play their game to the end.
They took the bandages, and cursing at his delay
They took the casks that might keep the fires on their ship at bay;
And they rowed back to *Nabara*, trailing their blood behind
Over the water, the sunset and crimson ebb of their day.

For two hours more they fought, while *Nabara* beneath their feet
Was turned to a heap of smouldering scrap-iron. Once again
The flames they had checked a while broke out. When the
                                        forward gun
Was hit, they turned about
Bringing the after gun to bear. They fought in pain
And the instant knowledge of death: but the waters filling
                                        their riven
Ship could not quench the love that fired them. As each man fell
To the deck, his body took fire as if death made visible
That burning spirit. For two more hours they fought, and at seven
They fired their last shell.

82

Of her officers all but one were dead. Of her engineers
All but one were dead. Of the fifty-two that had sailed
In her, all were dead but fourteen – and each of these half killed
With wounds. And the night-dew fell in a hush of ashen tears,
And *Nabara*'s tongue was stilled.
Southward the sheltering havens grew dark, the cliffs and the green
Shallows they knew; where their friends had watched them
                       as evening wore
To a glowing end, who swore
Nabara must show a white flag now, but saw instead the fourteen
Climb into their matchwood boat and fainting pull for the shore.

Canarias lowered a launch that swept in a greyhound's curve
Pitiless to pursue
And cut them off. But that bloodless and all-but-phantom crew
Still gave no soft concessions to fate: they strung their nerve
For one last fling of defiance, they shipped their oars and threw
Hand-grenades at the launch as it circled about to board them.
But the strength of the hands that had carved them a hold on history
Failed them at last: the grenades fell short of the enemy,
Who grappled and overpowered them,
While *Nabara* sank by the stern in the hushed Cantabrian sea.

                         *   *   *

They bore not a charmed life. They went into battle foreseeing
Probable loss, and they lost. The tides of Biscay flow
Over the obstinate bones of many, the winds are sighing
Round prison walls where the rest are doomed like their
                       ships to rust –
Men of the Basque country, the Mar Cantabrico.
Simple men who asked of their life no mythical splendour,
They loved its familiar ways so well that they preferred
In the rudeness of their heart to die rather than to surrender . . .
Mortal these words and the deed they remember, but cast a seed
Shall flower for an age when freedom is man's creative word.

Freedom was more than a word, more than the base coinage
Of politicians who hiding behind the skirts of peace
They had defiled, gave up that country to rack and carnage:
For whom, indelibly stamped with history's contempt,
Remains but to haunt the blackened shell of their policies.
For these I have told of, freedom was flesh and blood – a mortal
Body, the gun-breech hot to its touch: yet the battle's height
Raised it to love's meridian and held it awhile immortal;
And its light through time still flashes like a star's that has
                                        turned to ashes,
Long after *Nabara*'s passion was quenched in the sea's heart.

PASSAGE FROM CHILDHOOD

His earliest memory, the mood
Fingered and frail as maidenhair,
Was this – a china cup somewhere
In a green, deep wood.
He lives to find again somewhere
That wood, that homely cup; to taste all
Its chill, imagined dews; to dare
The dangerous crystal.

Who can say what misfeatured elf
First led him into that lifelong
Passage of mirrors where, so young,
He saw himself
Balanced as Blondin, more headstrong
Than baby Hercules, rare as a one-
Cent British Guiana, above the wrong
And common run?

He knew the secrecy of squirrels,
The foolish doves' antiphony,
And what wrens fear. He was gun-shy,
Hating all quarrels.

Life was a hostile land to spy,
Full of questions he dared not ask
Lest the answer in mockery
Or worse unmask.

Quick to injustice, quick he grew
This hermit and contorted shell.
Self-pity like a thin rain fell,
Fouling the view:
Then tree-trunks seemed wet roots of hell,
Wren or catkin might turn vicious,
The dandelion clock could tell
Nothing auspicious.

No exile has ever looked so glum
With the pines fretful overhead,
Yet he felt at home in the gothic glade –
More than at home.
You will forgive him that he played
Bumble-puppy on the small mossed lawn
All by himself for hours, afraid
Of being born.

Lying awake one night, he saw
Eternity stretched like a howl of pain:
He was tiny and terrible, a new pin
On a glacier's floor.
Very few they are who have lain
With eternity and lived to tell it:
There's a secret process in his brain
And he cannot sell it.

Now, beyond reach of sense or reason,
His life walks in a glacial sleep
For ever, since he drank that cup
And found it poison.

He's one more ghost, engaged to keep
Eternity's long hours and mewed
Up in live flesh with no escape
From solitude.

from WORD OVER ALL

THE ALBUM

I see you, a child
In a garden sheltered for buds and playtime,
Listening as if beguiled
By a fancy beyond your years and the flowering maytime.
The print is faded: soon there will be
No trace of that pose enthralling,
Nor visible echo of my voice distantly calling
'Wait! Wait for me!'

Then I turn the page
To a girl who stands like a questioning iris
By the waterside, at an age
That asks every mirror to tell what the heart's desire is.
The answer she finds in that oracle stream
Only time could affirm or disprove,
Yet I wish I was there to venture a warning, 'Love
Is not what you dream.'

Next, you appear
As if garlands of wild felicity crowned you –
Courted, caressed, you wear
Like immortelles the lovers and friends around you.
'They will not last you, rain or shine,
They are but straws and shadows,'
I cry: 'Give not to those charming desperadoes
What was made to be mine.'

One picture is missing –
The last. It would show me a tree stripped bare
By intemperate gales, her amazing
Noonday of blossom spoilt which promised so fair.

Yet, scanning those scenes at your heyday taken,
I tremble, as one who must view
In the crystal a doom he could never deflect – yes, I too
Am fruitlessly shaken.

I close the book;
But the past slides out of its leaves to haunt me
And it seems, wherever I look,
Phantoms of irreclaimable happiness taunt me.
Then I see her, petalled in new-blown hours,
Beside me – 'All you love most there
Has blossomed again,' she murmurs, 'all that you missed there
Has grown to be yours.'

DEPARTURE IN THE DARK

Nothing so sharply reminds a man he is mortal
As leaving a place
In a winter morning's dark, the air on his face
Unkind as the touch of sweating metal:
Simple goodbyes to children or friends become
A felon's numb
Farewell, and love that was a warm, a meeting place –
Love is the suicide's grave under the nettles.

Gloomed and clemmed as if by an imminent ice-age
Lies the dear world
Of your street-strolling, field-faring. The senses, curled
At the dead end of a shrinking passage,
Care not if close the inveterate hunters creep,
And memories sleep
Like mammoths in lost caves. Drear, extinct is the world,
And has no voice for consolation or presage.

There is always something at such times of the passover,
When the dazed heart
Beats for it knows not what, whether you part
From home or prison, acquaintance or lover –
Something wrong with the time-table, something unreal
In the scrambled meal
And the bag ready packed by the door, as though the heart
Has gone ahead, or is staying here for ever.

No doubt for the Israelites that early morning
It was hard to be sure
If home were prison or prison home: the desire
Going forth meets the desire returning.
This land, that had cut their pride down to the bone
Was now their own
By ancient deeds of sorrow. Beyond, there was nothing sure
But a desert of freedom to quench their fugitive yearnings.

At this blind hour the heart is informed of nature's
Ruling that man
Should be nowhere a more tenacious settler than
Among wry thorns and ruins, yet nurture
A seed of discontent in his ripest ease.
There's a kind of release
And a kind of torment in every goodbye for every man
And will be, even to the last of his dark departures.

CORNET SOLO

Thirty years ago lying awake,
Lying awake
In London at night when childhood barred me
From livelier pastimes, I'd hear a street-band break
Into old favourites – 'The Ash Grove', 'Killarney'
Or 'Angels Guard Thee'.

That was the music for such an hour –
A deciduous hour
Of leaf-wan drizzle, of solitude
And gaslight bronzing the gloom like an autumn flower –
The time and music for a boy imbrued
With the pensive mood.

I could have lain for hours together,
Sweet hours together,
Listening to the cornet's cry
Down wet streets gleaming like patent leather
Where beauties jaunted in cabs to their revelry,
Jewelled and spry.

Plaintive its melody rose or waned
Like an autumn wind
Blowing the rain on beds of aster,
On man's last bed: mournful and proud it complained
As a woman who dreams of the charms that graced her,
In young days graced her.

Strange how those yearning airs could sweeten
And still enlighten
The hours when solitude gave me her breast.
Strange they could tell a mere child how hearts may beat in
The self-same tune for the once-possessed
And the unpossessed.

Last night, when I heard a cornet's strain,
It seemed a refrain
Wafted from thirty years back – so remote an
Echo it bore: but I felt again
The prophetic mood of a child, too long forgotten,
Too lightly forgotten.

O DREAMS, O DESTINATIONS

1

For infants time is like a humming shell
Heard between sleep and sleep, wherein the shores
Foam-fringed, wind-fluted of the strange earth dwell
And the sea's cavernous hunger faintly roars.
It is the humming pole of summer lanes
Whose sound quivers like heat-haze endlessly
Over the corn, over the poppied plains –
An emanation from the earth or sky.
Faintly they hear, through the womb's lingering haze,
A rumour of that sea to which they are born:
They hear the ringing pole of summer days,
But need not know what hungers for the corn.
They are the lisping rushes in a stream –
Grace-notes of a profound, legato dream.

2

Children look down upon the morning-grey
Tissue of mist that veils a valley's lap:
Their fingers itch to tear it and unwrap
The flags, the roundabouts, the gala day.
They watch the spring rise inexhaustibly –
A breathing thread out of the eddied sand,
Sufficient to their day: but half their mind
Is on the sailed and glittering estuary.
Fondly we wish their mist might never break,
Knowing it hides so much that best were hidden:
We'd chain them by the spring, lest it should broaden
For them into a quicksand and a wreck.
But they slip through our fingers like the source,
Like mist, like time that has flagged out their course.

3

That was the fatal move, the ruination
Of innocence so innocently begun,
When in the lawless orchard of creation
The child left this fruit for that rosier one.
Reaching towards the far thing, we begin it;
Looking beyond, or backward, more and more
We grow unfaithful to the unique minute
Till, from neglect, its features stale and blur.
Fish, bird or beast was never thus unfaithful –
Man only casts the image of his joys
Beyond his senses' reach; and by this fateful
Act, he confirms the ambiguous power of choice.
Innocence made that first choice. It is she
Who weeps, a child chained to the outraged tree.

4

Our youthtime passes down a colonnade
Shafted with alternating light and shade.
All's dark or dazzle there. Half in a dream
Rapturously we move, yet half afraid
Never to wake. That diamond-point, extreme
Brilliance engraved on us a classic theme:
The shaft of darkness had its lustre too,
Rising where earth's concentric mysteries gleam.
Oh youth-charmed hours, that made an avenue
Of fountains playing us on to love's full view,
A cypress walk to some romantic grave –
Waking, how false in outline and in hue
We find the dreams that flickered on our cave:
Only your fire, which cast them, still seems true.

5

All that time there was thunder in the air:
Our nerves branched and flickered with summer lightning.
The taut crab-apple, the pampas quivering, the glare
On the roses seemed irrelevant, or a heightening

At most of the sealed-up hour wherein we awaited
What? – some explosive oracle to abash
The platitudes on the lawn? heaven's delegated
Angel – the golden rod, our burning bush?
No storm broke. Yet in retrospect the rose
Mounting vermilion, fading, glowing again
Like a fire's heart, that breathless inspiration
Of pampas grass, crab-tree's attentive pose
Never were so divinely charged as then –
The veiled Word's flesh, a near annunciation.

6

Symbols of gross experience! – our grief
Flowed, like a sacred river, underground:
Desire bred fierce abstractions on the mind,
Then like an eagle soared beyond belief.
Often we tried our breast against the thorn,
Our paces on the turf: whither we flew,
Why we should agonize, we hardly knew –
Nor what ached in us, asking to be born.
Ennui of youth! – thin air above the clouds,
Vain divination of the sunless stream
Mirror that impotence, till we redeem
Our birthright, and the shadowplay concludes.
Ah, not in dreams, but when our souls engage
With the common mesh and moil, we come of age.

7

Older, we build a road where once our active
Heat threw up mountains and the deep dales veined:
We're glad to gain the limited objective,
Knowing the war we fight in has no end.
The road must needs follow each contour moulded
By that fire in its losing fight with earth:
We march over our past, we may behold it
Dreaming a slave's dream on our bivouac hearth.
Lost the archaic dawn wherein we started,

The appetite for wholeness: now we prize
Half-loaves, half-truths – enough for the half-hearted,
The gleam snatched from corruption satisfies.
Dead youth, forgive us if, all but defeated,
We raise a trophy where your honour lies.

8

But look, the old illusion still returns,
Walking a field-path where the succory burns
Like summer's eye, blue lustre-drops of noon,
And the heart follows it and freshly yearns:
Yearns to the sighing distances beyond
Each height of happiness, the vista drowned
In gold-dust haze, and dreams itself immune
From change and night to which all else is bound.
Love, we have caught perfection for a day
As succory holds a gem of halcyon ray:
Summer burns out, its flower will tarnish soon –
Deathless illusion, that could so relay
The truth of flesh and spirit, sun and clay
Singing for once together all in tune!

9

To travel like a bird, lightly to view
Deserts where stone gods founder in the sand,
Ocean embraced in a white sleep with land;
To escape time, always to start anew.
To settle like a bird, make one devoted
Gesture of permanence upon the spray
Of shaken stars and autumns; in a bay
Beyond the crestfallen surges to have floated.
Each is our wish. Alas, the bird flies blind,
Hooded by a dark sense of destination:
Her weight on the glass calm leaves no impression,
Her home is soon a basketful of wind.
Travellers, we're fabric of the road we go;
We settle, but like feathers on time's flow.

THE POET

For me there is no dismay
Though ills enough impend.
I have learned to count each day
Minute by breathing minute –
Birds that lightly begin it,
Shadows muting its end –
As lovers count for luck
Their own heart-beats and believe
In the forest of time they pluck
Eternity's single leaf.

Tonight the moon's at the full.
Full moon's the time for murder.
But I look to the clouds that hide her –
The bay below me is dull,
An unreflecting glass –
And chafe for the clouds to pass,
And wish she suddenly might
Blaze down at me so I shiver
Into a twelve-branched river
Of visionary light.

For now imagination,
My royal, impulsive swan,
With raking flight – I can see her –
Comes down as it were upon
A lake in whirled snow-floss
And flurry of spray like a skier
Checking. Again I feel
The wounded waters heal.
Never before did she cross
My heart with such exaltation.

Oh, on this striding edge,
This hare-bell height of calm
Where intuitions swarm
Like nesting gulls and knowledge
Is free as the winds that blow,
A little while sustain me,
Love, till my answer is heard!
Oblivion roars below,
Death's cordon narrows: but vainly,
If I've slipped the carrier word.

Dying, any man may
Feel wisdom harmonious, fateful
At the tip of his dry tongue.
All I have felt or sung
Seems now but the moon's fitful
Sleep on a clouded bay,
Swan's maiden flight, or the climb
To a tremulous, hare-bell crest.
Love, tear the song from my breast!
Short, short is the time.

WATCHING POST

A hill flank overlooking the Axe valley.
Among the stubble a farmer and I keep watch
For whatever may come to injure our countryside –
Light-signals, parachutes, bombs, or sea-invaders.
The moon looks over the hill's shoulder, and hope
Mans the old ramparts of an English night.

In a house down there was Marlborough born. One night
Monmouth marched to his ruin out of that valley.
Beneath our castled hill, where Britons kept watch,
Is a church where the Drakes, old lords of this countryside,
Sleep under their painted effigies. No invaders
Can dispute their legacy of toughness and hope.

Two counties away, over Bristol, the searchlights hope
To find what danger is in the air tonight.
Presently gunfire from Portland reaches our valley
Tapping like an ill-hung door in a draught. My watch
Says nearly twelve. All over the countryside
Moon-dazzled men are peering out for invaders.

The farmer and I talk for a while of invaders:
But soon we turn to crops – the annual hope,
Making of cider, prizes for ewes. Tonight
How many hearts along this war-mazed valley
Dream of a day when at peace they may work and watch
The small sufficient wonders of the countryside.

Image or fact, we both in the countryside
Have found our natural law, and until invaders
Come will answer its need: for both of us, hope
Means a harvest from small beginnings, who this night
While the moon sorts out into shadow and shape our valley,
A farmer and a poet, are keeping watch.

July, 1940

WHERE ARE THE WAR POETS?

They who in folly or mere greed
Enslaved religion, markets, laws,
Borrow our language now and bid
Us to speak up in freedom's cause.

It is the logic of our times,
No subject for immortal verse –
That we who lived by honest dreams
Defend the bad against the worse.

WILL IT BE SO AGAIN?

Will it be so again
That the brave, the gifted are lost from view,
And empty, scheming men
Are left in peace their lunatic age to renew?
Will it be so again?

Must it be always so
That the best are chosen to fall and sleep
Like seeds, and we too slow
In claiming the earth they quicken, and the old usurpers reap
What they could not sow?

Will it be so again –
The jungle code and the hypocrite gesture?
A poppy wreath for the slain
And a cut-throat world for the living? that stale imposture
Played on us once again?

Will it be as before –
Peace, with no heart or mind to ensue it,
Guttering down to war
Like a libertine to his grave? We should not be surprised:
                                        we knew it
Happen before.

Shall it be so again?
Call not upon the glorious dead
To be your witnesses then.
The living alone can nail to their promise the ones who said
It shall not be so again.

THE INNOCENT

A forward child, a sullen boy,
My living image in the pool,
The glass that made me look a fool –
He was my judgement and my joy.

The bells that chimed above the lake,
The swans asleep in evening's eye,
Bright transfers pressed on memory
From him their gloss and anguish take.

When I was desolate, he came
A wizard way to charm my toys:
But when he heard a stranger's voice
He broke the toys, I bore the shame.

I built a house of crystal tears
Amid the myrtles for my friend:
He said, no man has ever feigned
Or kept the lustre of my years.

Later, a girl and I descried
His shadow on the fern-flecked hill,
His double near our bed: and still
The more I lived, the more he died.

Now a revenant slips between
The fine-meshed minutes of the clock
To weep the time we lost and mock
All that my desperate ditties mean.

JIG

That winter love spoke and we raised no objection, at
Easter 'twas daisies all light and affectionate,
June sent us crazy for natural selection – not
Four traction-engines could tear us apart.
Autumn then coloured the map of our land,
Oaks shuddered and apples came ripe to the hand,
In the gap of the hills we played happily, happily,
Even the moon couldn't tell us apart.

Grave winter drew near and said, 'This will not do at all –
If you continue, I fear you will rue it all.'
So at the New Year we vowed to eschew it
Although we both knew it would break our heart.
But spring made hay of our good resolutions –
Lovers, you may be as wise as Confucians,
Yet once love betrays you he plays you and plays you
Like fishes for ever, so take it to heart.

HORNPIPE

Now the peak of summer's past, the sky is overcast
And the love we swore would last for an age seems deceit:
Paler is the guelder since the day we first beheld her
In blush beside the elder drifting sweet, drifting sweet.

Oh quickly they fade – the sunny esplanade,
Speed-boats, wooden spades, and the dunes where we've lain:
Others will be lying amid the sea-pinks sighing
For love to be undying, and they'll sigh in vain.

It's hurrah for each night we have spent our love so lightly
And never dreamed there might be no more to spend at all.
It's goodbye to every lover who thinks he'll live in clover
All his life, for noon is over soon and night-dews fall.

If I could keep you there with the berries in your hair
And your lacy fingers fair as the may, sweet may,
I'd have no heart to do it, for to stay love is to rue it
And the harder we pursue it, the faster it's away.

THE REBUKE

Down in the lost and April days
What lies we told, what lies we told!
Nakedness seemed the one disgrace,
And there'd be time enough to praise
The truth when we were old.

The irresponsible poets sung
What came into their head:
Time to pick and choose among
The bold profusions of our tongue
When we were dead, when we were dead.

Oh wild the words we uttered then
In woman's ear, in woman's ear,
Believing all we promised when
Each kiss created earth again
And every far was near.

Little we guessed, who spoke the word
Of hope and freedom high
Spontaneously as wind or bird
To crowds like cornfields still or stirred,
It was a lie, a heart-felt lie.

Now the years advance into
A calmer stream, a colder stream,
We doubt the flame that once we knew,
Heroic words sound all untrue
As love-lies in a dream.

Yet fools are the old who won't be taught
Modesty by their youth:
That pandemonium of the heart,
That sensual arrogance did impart
A kind of truth, a kindling truth.

Where are the sparks at random sown,
The spendthrift fire, the holy fire?
Who cares a damn for truth that's grown
Exhausted haggling for its own
And speaks without desire?

from POEMS 1943–1947

THE DOUBLE VISION

The river this November afternoon
Rests in an equipoise of sun and cloud:
A glooming light, a gleaming darkness shroud
Its passage. All seems tranquil, all in tune.

Image and real are joined like Siamese twins:
Their doubles draw the willows, a brown mare
Drinks her reflection. There's no margin where
Substance leaves off, the illusory begins.

You and I by the river contemplate
Our ideal selves, glossed here, crystal-divined:
We yearn to them, knowing one sigh of wind
Will rub these precious figures from the slate.

It is not of their transience I'm afraid,
But thinking how most human loves protract
Themselves to unreality – the fact
Drained of its virtue by the image it made.

O double vision of the autumnal stream,
Teach me to bear love's fusion or diffusion!
O gems of purest water, pure illusion,
Answer my rays and cluster to a theme!

THE WOMAN ALONE

1

Take any place – this garden plot will do
Where he with mower, scythe or hook goes out
To fight the grass and lay a growing fever,
Volcanic for another, dead to me;
Meek is the ghost, a banked furnace the man.

107

Take any time – this autumn day will serve,
Ripe with grassed fruit, raw with departing wings,
When I, whom in my youth the season tempted
To oceanic amplitudes, bend down
And pick a rotting apple from the grass.

From every here and now a thread leads back
Through faithless seasons and devouring seas:
New blooms, dead leaves bury it not, nor combers
Break it – my life line and my clue: the same
That brought him safe out of a labyrinth.

So I, the consort of an absent mind,
The emerald lost in a green waste of time,
The castaway for whom all space is island –
To follow, find, escape, this thread in hand,
Warp myself out upon the swelling past.

2

Take any joy – the thread leads always on
To here and now: snow, silence, vertigo;
His frozen face, a woman who bewails not
Only because she fears one echoing word
May bring the avalanche about her ears.

Take any joy that was – here it remains,
Corruptless, irrecoverable, cold
As a dead smile, beneath the cruel glacier
That moved upon our kisses, lambs and leaves,
Stilled them, but will not let their forms dissolve.

O tomb transparent of my waxen joys!
O lifelike dead under the skin of ice!
O frozen face of love where my one treasure
Is locked, and the key lost! May I not share
Even the bare oblivion of your fate?

But dare I throw the past into one fire,
One burning cry to break the silence, break
The cataleptic snows, the dream of falling?
Last night I thought he stood beside my bed
And said, 'Wake up! You were dreaming. I am here.'

3

Take any grief – the maggot at the nerve,
The words that bore the skull like waterdrops,
The castaway's upon the foam-racked island,
The lurching figures of a mind's eclipse –
I have felt each and all as love decayed.

Yet every grief revives a fainting love.
They are love's children too; I live again
In them; my breast yearns to their innocent cruelty.
If only tears can float a stranded heart,
If only sighs can move it, I will grieve.

The pleasured nerve, the small-talk in the night,
The voyaging when isles were daisy-chains,
The dance of mere routine – if I could reach them
Again through this sick labyrinth of grief,
I would rejoice in it, to reach them so.

Alas, hull-down upon hope's ashen verge
Hastens the vessel that our joined hands launched,
Stretching my heart-strings out beyond endurance.
Ah, will they never snap? Can I not climb
The signal hill, and wave, and *mean* goodbye?

THE UNWANTED

On a day when the breath of roses
    Plumpened a swooning breeze
And all the silken combes of summer
    Opened wide their knees,
Between two sighs they planted one –
A willed one, a wanted one –
And he will be the sign, they said, of our felicities.

Eager the loins he sprang from,
    Happy the sheltering heart:
Seldom had the seed of man
    So charmed, so clear a start.
And he was born as frail a one,
As ailing, freakish, pale a one
As ever the wry planets knotted their beams to thwart.

Sun locked up for winter;
    Earth an empty rind:
Two strangers harshly flung together
    As by a flail of wind.
Oh was it not a furtive thing,
A loveless, damned, abortive thing –
This flurry of the groaning dust, and what it left behind!

Sure, from such warped beginnings
    Nothing debonair
Can come? But neither shame nor panic,
    Drugs nor sharp despair
Could uproot that untoward thing,
That all too fierce and froward thing:
Willy-nilly born it was, divinely formed and fair.

THE SITTING

(for Lawrence Gowing)*

So like a god I sit here,
One of those stone dreamers quarried from solitude,
A genius – if ever there was one – of the place:
The mountain's only child, lips aloof as a snow-line,
Forearms impassive along the cloud-base of aeons,
Eyes heavy on distance –
Graven eyes that flinch not, flash not, if eagles
Clap their wings in my face.

With hieratic gestures
He the suppliant, priest, interpreter, subtly
Wooing my virtue, officiates by the throne.
I know the curious hands are shaping, reshaping the image
Of what is only an image of things impalpable.
I feel how the eyes strain
To catch a truth behind the oracular presence –
Eyes that augur through stone.

And the god asks, 'What have I for you
But the lichenous shadow of thought veiling my temple,
The runnels a million time-drops have chased on my cheek?'
And the man replies, 'I will show you the creed of your bone, I'll
                                        draw you
The shape of solitude to which you were born.'
And the god cries, 'I am meek,
Brushed by an eagle's wing; and a voice bids me
Speak. But I cannot speak.'

The god thinks, Let him project, if
He must, his passionate shapings on my stone heart,
Wrestle over my body with his sprite,
Through these blind eyes imagine a skin-deep world in perspective:

*The portrait by Sir Lawrence Gowing (1946) appears on the cover.

111

Let him make, if he will, the crypt of my holy mountain
His own: let even the light
That bathes my temple become as it were an active
Property of his sight.

O man, O innocent artist
Who paint me with green of your fields, with amber or yellow
Of love's hair, red of the heart's blood, eyebright blue,
Conjuring forms and rainbows out of an empty mist –
Your hand is upon me, as even now you follow
Along the immortal clue
Threading my veins of emerald, topaz, amethyst,
And know not it ends in you.

STATUETTE: LATE MINOAN

Girl of the musing mouth,
The mild archaic air,
For whom do you subtly smile?
Yield to what power or prayer
Breasts vernally bare?

I seem to be peering at you
Through the wrong end of time
That shrinks to a bright, far image –
Great Mother of earth's prime –
A stature sublime.

So many golden ages
Of sunshine steeped your clay,
So dear did the maker cherish
In you life's fostering ray,
That you warm us today.

Goddess or girl, you are earth.
The smile, the offered breast –
They were the dream of one
Thirsting as I for rest,
As I, unblest.

IS IT FAR TO GO?*

Is it far to go?
   A step – no further.
Is it hard to go?
   Ask the melting snow,
   The eddying feather.

What can I take there?
   Not a hank, not a hair.
What shall I leave behind?
   Ask the hastening wind,
   The fainting star.

Shall I be gone long?
   For ever and a day.
To whom there belong?
   Ask the stone to say,
   Ask my song.

Who will say farewell?
   The beating bell.
Will anyone miss me?
   That I dare not tell –
   Quick, Rose, and kiss me.

* The third stanza is on CDL's tombstone in Dorset.

EMILY BRONTË

All is the same still. Earth and heaven locked in
A wrestling dream the seasons cannot break:
Shrill the wind tormenting my obdurate thorn trees,
Moss-rose and stone-chat silent in its wake.
Time has not altered here the rhythms I was rocked in,
Creation's throb and ache.

All is yet the same, for mine was a country
Stoic, unregenerate, beyond the power
Of man to mollify or God to disburden –
An ingrown landscape none might long endure
But one who could meet with a passion wilder-wintry
The scalding breath of the moor.

All is yet the same as when I roved the heather
Chained to a demon through the shrieking night,
Took him by the throat while he flailed my sibylline
Assenting breast, and won him to delight.
O truth and pain immortally bound together!
O lamp the storm made bright!

Still on those heights prophetic winds are raving,
Heath and harebell intone a plainsong grief:
'Shrink, soul of man, shrink into your valleys –
Too sharp that agony, that spring too brief!
Love, though your love is but the forged engraving
Of hope on a stricken leaf!'

Is there one whom blizzards warm and rains enkindle
And the bitterest furnace could no more refine?
Anywhere one too proud for consolation,
Burning for pure freedom so that he will pine,
Yes, to the grave without her? Let him mingle
His barren dust with mine.

But is there one who faithfully has planted
His seed of light in the heart's deepest scar?
When the night is darkest, when the wind is keenest,
He, he shall find upclimbing from afar
Over his pain my chaste, my disenchanted
And death-rebuking star.

BIRTHDAY POEM FOR THOMAS HARDY

Is it birthday weather for you, dear soul?
Is it fine your way,
With tall moon-daisies alight, and the mole
Busy, and elegant hares at play
By meadow paths where once you would stroll
In the flush of day?

I fancy the beasts and flowers there beguiled
By a visitation
That casts no shadow, a friend whose mild
Inquisitive glance lights with compassion,
Beyond the tomb, on all of this wild
And humbled creation.

It's hard to believe a spirit could die
Of such generous glow,
Or to doubt that somewhere a bird-sharp eye
Still broods on the capers of men below,
A stern voice asks the Immortals why
They should plague us so.

Dear poet, wherever you are, I greet you.
Much irony, wrong,
Innocence you'd find here to tease or entreat you,
And many the fate-fires have tempered strong,
But none that in ripeness of soul could meet you
Or magic of song.

Great brow, frail frame – gone. Yet you abide
In the shadow and sheen,
All the mellowing traits of a countryside
That nursed your tragi-comical scene;
And in us, warmer-hearted and brisker-eyed
Since you have been.

A HARD FROST

A frost came in the night and stole my world
And left this changeling for it – a precocious
Image of spring, too brilliant to be true:
White lilac on the windowpane, each grass-blade
Furred like a catkin, maydrift loading the hedge.
The elms behind the house are elms no longer
But blossomers in crystal, stems of the mist
That hangs yet in the valley below, amorphous
As the blind tissue whence creation formed.
    The sun looks out, and the fields blaze with diamonds.
Mockery spring, to lend this bridal gear
For a few hours to a raw country maid,
Then leave her all disconsolate with old fairings
Of aconite and snowdrop! No, not here
Amid this flounce and filigree of death
Is the real transformation scene in progress,
But deep below where frost
Worrying the stiff clods unclenches their
Grip on the seed and lets our future breathe.

THE CHRISTMAS TREE

Put out the lights now!
Look at the Tree, the rough tree dazzled
In oriole plumes of flame,
Tinselled with twinkling frost fire, tasselled

116

With stars and moons – the same
That yesterday hid in the spinney and had no fame
Till we put out the lights now.

Hard are the nights now:
The fields at moonrise turn to agate,
Shadows are cold as jet;
In dyke and furrow, in copse and faggot
The frost's tooth is set;
And stars are the sparks whirled out by the north wind's fret
On the flinty nights now.

So feast your eyes now
On mimic star and moon-cold bauble:
Worlds may wither unseen,
But the Christmas Tree is a tree of fable,
A phoenix in evergreen,
And the world cannot change or chill what its mysteries mean
To your hearts and eyes now.

The vision dies now
Candle by candle: the tree that embraced it
Returns to its own kind,
To be earthed again and weather as best it
May the frost and the wind.
Children, it too had its hour – you will not mind
If it lives or dies now.

THE NEUROTIC

The spring came round, and still he was not dead.
Skin of the earth deliciously powdered
With buttercups and daisies – oh, Proserpina
Refreshed by sleep, wild-cherry-garlanded
And laughing in the sallies of the willow-wren!
With lambs and lilies spring came round again.

117

Who would suppose, seeing him walk the meadows,
He walks a treadmill there, grinding himself
To powder, dust to greyer dust, or treads
An invisible causeway lipped by chuckling shadows?
Take his arm if you like, you'll not come near him.
His mouth is an ill-stitched wound opening: hear him.

'I will not lift mine eyes unto the hills
For there white lambs nuzzle and creep like maggots.
I will not breathe the lilies of the valley
For through their scent a chambered corpse exhales.
If a petal floats to earth, I am oppressed.
The grassblades twist, twist deep in my breast.'

The night came on, and he was still alive.
Lighted tanks of streets a-swarm with denizens
Darting to trysts, sauntering to parties.
How all the heart-fires twinkle! Yes, they thrive
In the large illusion of freedom, in love's net
Where even the murderer can act and the judge regret.

This man who turns a phrase and twiddles a glass
Seems far from that pale muttering magician
Pent in a vicious circle of dilemmas.
But could you lift his blue, thick gaze and pass
Behind, you would walk a stage where endlessly
Phantoms rehearse unactable tragedy.

'In free air captive, in full day benighted,
I am as one for ever out of his element
Transparently enwombed, who from a bathysphere
Observes, wistful, amazed, but more affrighted,
Gay fluent forms of life weaving around,
And dares not break the bubble and be drowned.'

His doomsdays crawled like lava, till at length
All impulse clogged, the last green lung consumed,
Each onward step required the sweat of nightmare,
Each human act a superhuman strength . . .
And the guillemot, clotted with oil, droops her head.
And the mouse between the elastic paws shams dead.

Death mask of a genius unborn:
Tragic prince of a rejected play:
Soul of suffering that bequeathed no myth:
A dark tower and a never-sounded horn. –
Call him what we will, words cannot ennoble
This Atlas who fell down under a bubble.

SEEN FROM THE TRAIN

Somewhere between Crewkerne
And Yeovil it was. On the left of the line
Just as the crinkled hills unroll
To the plain. A church on a small green knoll –
A limestone church,
And above the church
Cedar boughs stretched like hands that yearn
To protect or to bless. The whole

Stood up, antique and clear
As a cameo, from the vale. I swear
It was not a dream. Twice, thrice had I found it
Chancing to look as my train wheeled round it.
But this time I passed,
Though I gazed as I passed
All the way down the valley, that knoll was not there,
Nor the church, nor the trees it mounded.

What came between to unsight me? . . .
But suppose, only suppose there might be
A secret look in a landscape's eye
Following you as you hasten by,
And you have your chance –
Two or three chances
At most – to hold and interpret it rightly,
Or it is gone for aye.

There was a time when men
Would have called it a vision, said that sin
Had blinded me since to a heavenly fact.
Well, I have neither invoked nor faked
Any church in the air,
And little I care
Whether or no I shall see it again.
But blindly my heart is racked

When I think how, not twice or thrice,
But year after year in another's eyes
I have caught the look that I missed today
Of the church, the knoll, the cedars – a ray
Of the faith, too, they stood for,
The hope they were food for,
The love they prayed for, facts beyond price –
And turned my eyes away.

IN THE SHELTER

In a shelter one night, when death was taking the air
Outside, I saw her, seated apart – a child
Nursing her doll, to one man's vision enisled
With radiance which might have shamed even death to its lair.

Then I thought of our Christmas roses at home – the dark
Lanterns comforting us a winter through
With the same dusky flush, the same bold spark
Of confidence, O sheltering child, as you.

Genius could never paint the maternal pose
More deftly than accident had roughed it there,
Setting amidst our terrors, against the glare
Of unshaded bulb and whitewashed brick, that rose.

Instinct was hers, and an earthquake hour revealed it
In flesh – the meek-laid lashes, the glint in the eye
Defying wrath and reason, the arms that shielded
A plaster doll from an erupting sky.

No argument for living could long sustain
These ills: it needs a faithful eye, to have seen all
Love in the droop of a lash and tell it eternal
By one pure bead of its dew-dissolving chain.

Dear sheltering child, if again misgivings grieve me
That love is only a respite, an opal bloom
Upon our snow-set fields, come back to revive me
Cradling your spark through blizzard, drift and tomb.

THE GRAVEYARD BY THE SEA*

(from Paul Valéry)

This quiet roof, where dove-sails saunter by,
Between the pines, the tombs, throbs visibly.
Impartial noon patterns the sea in flame –
That sea for ever starting and re-starting.
When thought has had its hour, oh how rewarding
Are the long vistas of celestial calm!

* The graveyard is at Sète (Hérault)

What grace of light, what pure toil goes to form
The manifold diamond of the elusive foam!
What peace I feel begotten at that source!
When sunlight rests upon a profound sea,
Time's air is sparkling, dream is certainty –
Pure artifice both of an eternal Cause.

Sure treasure, simple shrine to intelligence,
Palpable calm, visible reticence,
Proud-lidded water, Eye wherein there wells
Under a film of fire such depth of sleep –
O silence! . . . Mansion in my soul, you slope
Of gold, roof of a myriad golden tiles.

Temple of time, within a brief sigh bounded,
To this rare height inured I climb, surrounded
By the horizons of a sea-girt eye.
And, like my supreme offering to the gods,
That peaceful coruscation only breeds
A loftier indifference on the sky.

Even as a fruit's absorbed in the enjoying,
Even as within the mouth its body dying
Changes into delight through dissolution,
So to my melted soul the heavens declare
All bounds transfigured into a boundless air,
And I breathe now my future's emanation.

Beautiful heaven, true heaven, look how I change!
After such arrogance, after so much strange
Idleness – strange, yet full of potency –
I am all open to these shining spaces;
Over the homes of the dead my shadow passes,
Ghosting along – a ghost subduing me.

My soul laid bare to your midsummer fire,
O just, impartial light whom I admire,
Whose arms are merciless, you have I stayed
And give back, pure, to your original place.
Look at yourself . . . But to give light implies
No less a sombre moiety of shade.

Oh, for myself alone, mine, deep within
At the heart's quick, the poem's fount, between
The void and its pure issue, I beseech
The intimations of my secret power.
O bitter, dark and echoing reservoir
Speaking of depths always beyond my reach.

But know you – feigning prisoner of the boughs,
Gulf which eats up their slender prison-bars,
Secret which dazzles though mine eyes are closed –
What body drags me to its lingering end,
What mind draws *it* to this bone-peopled ground?
A star broods there on all that I have lost.

Closed, hallowed, full of insubstantial fire,
Morsel of earth to heaven's light given o'er –
This plot, ruled by its flambeaux, pleases me –
A place all gold, stone and dark wood, where shudders
So much marble above so many shadows:
And on my tombs, asleep, the faithful sea.

Keep off the idolaters, bright watch-dog, while –
A solitary with the shepherd's smile –
I pasture long my sheep, my mysteries,
My snow-white flock of undisturbéd graves!
Drive far away from here the careful doves,
The vain daydreams, the angels' questioning eyes!

Now present here, the future takes its time.
The brittle insect scrapes at the dry loam;
All is burnt up, used up, drawn up in air
To some ineffably rarefied solution . . .
Life is enlarged, drunk with annihilation,
And bitterness is sweet, and the spirit clear.

The dead lie easy, hidden in earth where they
Are warmed and have their mysteries burnt away.
Motionless noon, noon aloft in the blue
Broods on itself – a self-sufficient theme.
O rounded dome and perfect diadem,
I am what's changing secretly in you.

I am the only medium for your fears.
My penitence, my doubts, my baulked desires –
These are the flaw within your diamond pride . . .
But in their heavy night, cumbered with marble,
Under the roots of trees a shadow people
Has slowly now come over to your side.

To an impervious nothingness they're thinned,
For the red clay has swallowed the white kind;
Into the flowers that gift of life has passed.
Where are the dead? – their homely turns of speech,
The personal grace, the soul informing each?
Grubs thread their way where tears were once composed.

The bird-sharp cries of girls whom love is teasing,
The eyes, the teeth, the eyelids moistly closing,
The pretty breast that gambles with the flame,
The crimson blood shining when lips are yielded,
The last gift, and the fingers that would shield it –
All go to earth, go back into the game.

And you, great soul, is there yet hope in you
To find some dream without the lying hue
That gold or wave offers to fleshy eyes?
Will you be singing still when you're thin air?
All perishes. A thing of flesh and pore
Am I. Divine impatience also dies.

Lean immortality, all crêpe and gold,
Laurelled consoler frightening to behold,
Death is a womb, a mother's breast, you feign –
The fine illusion, oh the pious trick!
Who does not know them, and is not made sick –
That empty skull, that everlasting grin?

Ancestors deep down there, O derelict heads
Whom such a weight of spaded earth o'erspreads,
Who *are* the earth, in whom our steps are lost,
The real flesh-eater, worm unanswerable
Is not for you that sleep under the table:
Life is his meat, and I am still his host.

'Love', shall we call him? 'Hatred of self', maybe?
His secret tooth is so intimate with me
That any name would suit him well enough,
Enough that he can see, will, daydream, touch –
My flesh delights him, even upon my couch
I live but as a morsel of his life.

Zeno, Zeno, cruel philosopher Zeno,
Have you then pierced me with your feathered arrow
That hums and flies, yet does not fly! The sounding
Shaft gives me life, the arrow kills. Oh, sun! –
Oh, what a tortoise-shadow to outrun
My soul, Achilles' giant stride left standing!

No, no! Arise! The future years unfold.
Shatter, O body, meditation's mould!
And, O my breast, drink in the wind's reviving!
A freshness, exhalation of the sea,
Restores my soul . . . Salt-breathing potency!
Let's run at the waves and be hurled back to living!

Yes, mighty sea with such wild frenzies gifted
(The panther skin and the rent chlamys), sifted
All over with sun-images that glisten,
Creature supreme, drunk on your own blue flesh,
Who in a tumult like the deepest hush
Bite at your sequin-glittering tail – yes, listen!

The wind is rising! . . . We must try to live!
The huge air opens and shuts my book: the wave
Dares to explode out of the rocks in reeking
Spray. Fly away, my sun-bewildered pages!
Break, waves! Break up with your rejoicing surges
This quiet roof where sails like doves were pecking.

1948

from AN ITALIAN VISIT

FLIGHT TO ITALY

The winged bull trundles to the wired perimeter.
Cumbrously turns. Shivers, brakes clamped,
Bellowing four times, each engine tested
With routine ritual. Advances to the runway.
Halts again as if gathering heart
Or warily snuffing for picador cross-winds.
Then, then, a roar open-throated
Affronts the arena. Then fast, faster
Drawn by the magnet of his *idée fixe*,
Head down, tail up, he's charging the horizon.
      And the grass of the airfield grows smooth as a fur.
The runway's elastic and we the projectile;
Installations control-tower mechanics parked aeroplanes –
Units all woven to a ribbon unreeling,
Concrete melts and condenses to an abstract
Blur, and our blood thickens to think of
Rending, burning, as suburban terraces
Make for us, wave after wave.
                        The moment
Of Truth is here. We can only trust,
Being as wholly committed to other hands
As a babe at birth, Europa to the bull god.
And as when one dies in his sleep, there's no divining
The instant of take-off, so we who were earth-bound
Are air-borne, it seems, in the same breath.
The neutered terraces subside beneath us.

    Bank and turn, bank and turn,
Air-treading bull, my silver Alitalia!
Bank and turn, while the earth below
Swings like a dial on the wing-tip's axis,
Whirls and checks like a wheel of chance!

Now keep your course! On azure currents
Let the wings lift and sidle drowsily –
A halcyon rocked by the ghost of the gale.
To watchers in Kent you appear as a quicksilver
Bead skimming down the tilted sky;
To the mild-eyed aircrew, an everyday office:
To us, immured in motion, you mean
A warm womb pendant between two worlds.
        O trance prenatal and angelic transport!
Like embryos curled in this aluminium belly –
Food and oxygen gratis – again
We taste the pure freedom of the purely submissive,
The passive dominion of the wholly dependent.
Through heaven's transparent mysteries we travel
With a humdrum of engines, the mother's heartbeat:
And our foreshadowed selves begin to take shape, to be
Dimly adapted to their destination.
What migrant fancies this journeying generates! –
Almost we imagine a metempsychosis.

        Over the Channel now, beneath the enchanting
Inane babble of a baby-blue sky,
We soar through cloudland, at the heights of nonsense.
From a distance they might be sifted-sugar-drifts,
Meringues, iced cakes, confections of whipped cream
Lavishly piled for some Olympian party –
A child's idea of heaven. Now radiant
All around the airscrew's boring penumbra
The clouds redouble, as nearer we climb,
Their toppling fantasy. We skirt the fringe of icebergs,
Dive under eiderdowns, disport with snowmen
On fields of melting snow dinted by the wind's feet,
Gleefully brush past atom-bomb cauliflowers,
Frozen fuffs of spray from naval gunfire.
        Wool-gathering we fly through a world of make-believe.
We *are* the aircraft, the humming-bird hawk moth
Hovering and sipping at each cloud corolla;

130

But also ourselves, to whom these white follies are
Valid as symbols for a tonic reverie
Or as symptoms of febrile flight from the real.
Let us keep, while we can, the holiday illusion,
The heart's altimeter dancing bliss-high,
Forgetting gravity, regardless of earth
Out of sight, out of mind, like a menacing letter
Left at home in a drawer – let the next-of-kin acknowledge it.

  The cloud-floor is fissured suddenly. Clairvoyance
It seems, not sight, when the solid air frays and parts
Unveiling, like some rendezvous remote in a crystal,
Bright, infinitesimal, a fragment of France.
We scan the naked earth as it were through a skylight:
Down there, what life-size encounters, what industrious
Movement and vocations manifold go forward!
But to us, irresponsible, above the battle,
Villages and countryside reveal no more life than
A civilization asleep beneath a glacier,
Toy bricks abandoned on a plain of linoleum . . .
  After a hard winter, on the first warm day
The invalid venturing out into the rock-garden,
Pale as a shaft of December sunshine, pauses,
All at sea among the aubretia, the alyssum
And arabis – halts and moves on how warily,
As if to take soundings where the blossom foams and tumbles:
But what he does sound is the depth of his own weakness
At last, as never when pain-storms lashed him.
So we, convalescent from routine's long fever,
Plummeting our gaze down to river and plain,
Question if indeed that dazzling world beneath us
Be truth or delirium; and finding still so tentative
The answer, can gauge how nearly we were ghosts,
How far we must travel yet to flesh and blood.

But now the engines have quickened their beat
And the fuselage pulsates, panting like a fugitive.
Below us – oh, look at it! – earth has become
Sky, a thunderscape curdling to indigo,
Veined with valleys of green fork-lightning.
The atrocious Alps are upon us. Their ambush –
A primeval huddle, then a bristling and heaving of
Brutal boulder-shapes, an uprush of Calibans –
Unmasks its white-fanged malice to maul us.
The cabin grows colder. Keep height, my angel!
Where we are, all but terra firma is safe.
　　　Recall how flyers from a raid returning,
Lightened of one death, were elected for another:
Their homing thoughts too far ahead, a mountain
Stepped from the mist and slapped them down.
We, though trivial the hazard, retract
Our trailing dreams until we have cleared these ranges.
Exalted, numinous, aloof no doubt
To the land-locked vision, for us they invoke
A mood more intimate, a momentary flutter and
Draught of danger – death's fan coquettishly
Tapping the cheek ere she turn to dance elsewhere.
Our mien is the bolder for this mild flirtation,
Our eyes the brighter, since every brush with her
Gives flesh a souvenir, a feel of resurrection.

　　　Those peaks o'erpassed, we glissade at last to
A gentian pasture, the Genoan sea.
Look south, sky-goers! In flying colours
A map's unrolled there – the Italy
Your schooldays scanned once: the hills are sand-blond,
A pale green stands for the littoral plain:
The sea's bedizened with opening islands
Like iris eyes on a peacock's fan.
How slowly dawns on the drowsy newborn
Whose world's unworn yet – a firelit dress,
An ego's glamorous shell, a womb of rumours –

The first faint glimmering of otherness!
But half awake, we could take this country
For some vague drift from prenatal dreams:
Those hills and headlands, like sleep's projections
Or recollections, mere symbol seem.
        Then hurtling southward along shores of myrtle,
Silverly circle the last lap,
My bull-headed moth! This land is nothing
But a mythical name on an outline map
For us, till we've scaled it to our will's dimensions,
Filled in each wayward, imperious route,
Shaded it in with delays and chagrins,
Traced our selves over it, foot by foot.
Now tighter we circle, as if the vertical
Air is a whirlpool drawing us down;
And the airfield, a candle-bright pinpoint, invites us
To dance ere alighting . . . Hurry! We burn
For Rome so near us, for the phoenix moment
When we have thrown off this traveller's trance,
And mother-naked and ageless-ancient
Wake in her warm nest of renaissance.

from PEGASUS

PEGASUS

(In memoriam: L. B. L.) *

It was there on the hillside, no tall traveller's story.
A cloud caught on a whin-bush; an airing of bleached
Linen, a swan, the cliff of a marble quarry –
It could have been any of these: but as he approached,
He saw that it was indeed what he had cause
Both to doubt and believe in – a horse, a winged white horse.

It filled the pasture with essence of solitude.
The wind tiptoed away like an interloper,
The sunlight there became a transparent hood
Estranging what it revealed; and the bold horse-coper,
The invincible hero, trudging up Helicon,
Knew he had never before been truly alone.

It stood there, solid as ivory, dreamy as smoke;
Or moved, and its hooves went dewdropping so lightly
That even the wild cyclamen were not broken:
But when those hooves struck rock, such was their might
They tapped a crystal vein which flowed into song
As it ran through thyme and grasses down-along.

'Pegasus,' he called, 'Pegasus' – with the surprise
Of one for the first time naming his naked lover.
The creature turned its lordly, incurious eyes
Upon the young man; but they seemed to pass him over
As something beneath their pride or beyond their ken.
It returned to cropping the violets and cyclamen.

* LBL was the poet Lilian Bowes Lyon.

Such meekness, indifference frightened him more than any
Rumoured Chimaera. He wavered, remembering how
This milk-white beast was born from the blood of uncanny
Medusa, the nightmare-eyed: and at once, although
Its brief glance had been mild, he felt a cringing
And pinched himself to make sure he was not changing

Into a stone. The animal tossed its head;
The white mane lifted and fell like an arrogant whinny.
'Horses are meant to be ridden,' the hero said,
'Wings or no wings, and men to mount them. Athene
'Ordered my mission, besides, and certainly you
'Must obey that goddess,' he cried, and flung the lassoo.

The cyclamen bow their heads, the cicadas pause.
The mountain shivers from flank to snowy top,
Shaking off eagles as a pastured horse
Shakes off a cloud of flies. The faint airs drop.
Pegasus, with a movement of light on water,
Shimmers aside, is elsewhere, mocking the halter.

So there began the contest. A young man
Challenging, coaxing, pursuing, always pursuing
The dream of those dewfall hooves: a horse which ran
Quicksilver from his touch, sliding and slewing
Away, then immobile a moment, derisively tame,
Almost as if it entered into a game.

He summoned up his youth, his conscious art
To tire or trick the beast, criss-crossing the meadow
With web of patient moves, circling apart,
Nearing, and pouncing, but only upon its shadow.
What skill and passion weave the subtle net!
But Pegasus goes free, unmounted yet.

All day he tried for this radiant creature. The more he
Persevered, the less he thought of the task
For which he required it, and the ultimate glory.
So it let him draw close, closer – nearly to grasp
Its mane; but that instant it broke out wings like a spread
Of canvas, and sailed off easily overhead.

He cursed Pegasus then. Anger arose
With a new desire, as if it were some white girl
To stretch, mount, master, exhaust in shuddering throes.
The animal gave him a different look: it swirled
Towards him, circled him round in a dazzling mist,
And one light hoof just knocked upon his breast.

The pale sky yawns to its uttermost concave,
Flowers open their eyes, rivulets prance
Again, and over the mountainside a wave
Of sparkling air tumbles. Now from its trance
That holy ground is deeply sighing and stirring.
The heights take back their eagles, cicadas are whirring.

The furious art, the pursuer's rhythmic pace
Failed in him now. Another self had awoken,
Which knew – but felt no chagrin, no disgrace –
That he, not the winged horse, was being broken:
It was his lode, his lord, his appointed star,
He but its shadow and familiar.

So he lay down to sleep. Argos, Chimaera,
Athene in one solution were immersed.
Around him, on bush and blade, each dewdrop mirrored
A star, his riding star, his universe,
While on the moonlit flowers at his side
Pegasus grazed, palpable, undenied.

A golden bridle came to him in sleep –
A mesh of immortal fire and sensual earth,
Pliant as love, compulsive as the sweep
Of light-years, brilliant as truth, perfect as death.
He dreamed a magic bridle, and next day
When he awoke, there to his hand it lay.

Wings furled, on printless feet through the dews of morn
Pegasus stepped, in majesty and submission,
Towards him. Mane of tempest, delicate mien,
It was all brides, all thoroughbreds, all pent passion.
Breathing flowers upon him, it arched a superb
Neck to receive the visionary curb.

Pegasus said, 'The bridle that you found
'In sleep, you yourself made. Your hard pursuit,
'Your game with me upon this hallowed ground
'Forged it, your failures tempered it. I am brute
'And angel. He alone, who taps the source
'Of both, can ride me. Bellerophon, I am yours.'

THE COMMITTEE

So the committee met again, and again
Nailed themselves to the never-much-altered agenda,
Making their points as to the manner born,
Hammering them home with the skill of long practice.

These men and women are certainly representative
Of every interest concerned. For example, A. wears
Integrity like a sheriff's badge, while B.
Can grind an axe on either side of a question:
C. happens to have the facts, D. a vocation
For interpreting facts to the greater glory of Dogma:
E. is pompously charming, diffidently earnest,
F. is the acid-drop, the self-patented catalyst.
Our chairman's a prince of procedure, in temporizing

140

Power a Proteus, and adept in seeming to follow
Where actually he leads – as indeed he must be,
Or the rest would have torn him to pieces a long time ago.
Yet all, in a curious way, are public-spirited,
Groping with their *ad hoc* decisions to find
The missing, presumed omnipotent, directive.

Idly the sun tracing upon their papers
Doodles of plane-leaf shadows and rubbing them out:
The buzz of flies, the gen of the breeze, the river
Endlessly stropping its tides against the embankment:
Seasons revolving with colours like stage armies,
Years going west along the one-way street –
All these they ignore, whose session or obsession
Must do with means, not ends. But who called this meeting
Of irreconcilables? Will they work out some positive
Policy, something more than a *modus vivendi*?
Or be adjourned, *sine die*, their task half done?

So the committee, as usual, reached a compromise –
If reach is the word, denoting, as it ought to,
A destination (though why should destiny not
Favour a compromise, which is only the marriage
For better or worse between two or more incompatibles,
Like any marriage of minds?) and left the table,
There being no further business for today.
And the silent secretary wrote up the minutes,
Putting the leaves in order. For what? the eye
Of higher authority? or the seal of the dust?
Or again, to be dispersed irreparably
When the hinge turns and a brusque new life blows in?
And I regret another afternoon wasted,
And wearily think there is something to be said
For the methods of the dictatorships – I who shall waste
Even the last drops of twilight in self-pity
That I should have to be chairman, secretary,
And all the committee, all the one-man committee.

THE WRONG ROAD

There was no precise point at which to say
'I am on the wrong road.' So well he knew
Where he wanted to go, he had walked in a dream
Never dreaming he could lose his way.
Besides, for such travellers it's all but true
That up to a point any road will do
As well as another – so why not walk
Straight on? The trouble is, *after* this point
There's no turning back, not even a fork;
And you never can see that point until
After you have passed it. And when you know
For certain you are lost, there's nothing to do
But go on walking your road, although
You walk in a nightmare now, not a dream.

But are there no danger-signs? Couldn't he see
Something strange about the landscape to show
That he was near where he should not be?
Rather the opposite – perhaps the view
Gave him a too familiar look
And made him feel at home where he had no right
Of way. But when you have gone so far,
A landscape says less than it used to do
And nothing seems very strange. He might
Have noticed how, mile after mile, this road
Made easier walking – noticed a lack
Of grit and gradient; *there* was a clue.
Ah yes, if only he had listened to his feet!
But, as I told you, he walked in a dream.

You can argue it thus or thus: either the road
Changed gradually under his feet and became
A wrong road, or else it was he who changed
And put the road wrong. We'd hesitate to blame
The traveller for a highway's going askew:

142

Yet possibly he and it became one
At a certain stage, like means and ends.
For this lost traveller, all depends
On how real the road is to him – not as a mode
Of advancement or exercise – rather, as grain
To timber, intrinsic-real.
                                    He can but pursue
His course and believe that, granting the road
Was right at the start, it will see him through
Their errors and turn into the right road again.

ALMOST HUMAN

The man you know, assured and kind,
Wearing fame like an old tweed suit –
You would not think he has an incurable
Sickness upon his mind.

Finely that tongue, for the listening people,
Articulates love, enlivens clay;
While under his valued skin there crawls
An outlaw and a cripple.

Unenviable the renown he bears
When all's awry within? But a soul
Divinely sick may be immunized
From the scourge of common cares.

A woman weeps, a friend's betrayed,
Civilization plays with fire –
His grief or guilt is easily purged
In a rush of words to the head.

The newly dead, and their waxwork faces
With the look of things that could never have lived,
He'll use to prime his cold, strange heart
And prompt the immortal phrases.

Before you condemn this eminent freak
As an outrage upon mankind,
Reflect: something there is in him
That must for ever seek

To share the condition it glorifies,
To shed the skin that keeps it apart,
To bury its grace in a human bed –
And it walks on knives, on knives.

FINAL INSTRUCTIONS

For sacrifice, there are certain principles –
Few, but essential.

I do not mean your ritual. This you have learnt –
The garland, the salt, a correct use of the knife,
And what to do with the blood:
Though it is worth reminding you that no two
Sacrifices ever turn out alike –
Not where this god is concerned.

The celebrant's approach may be summed up
In three words – patience, joy,
Disinterestedness. Remember, you do not sacrifice
For your own glory or peace of mind:
You are there to assist the clients and please the god.

It goes without saying
That only the best is good enough for the god.
But the best – I must emphasize it – even your best
Will by no means always be found acceptable.
Do not be discouraged:
Some lizard or passing cat may taste your sacrifice
And bless the god: it will not be entirely wasted.

But the crucial point is this:
You are called only to *make* the sacrifice.
Whether or no he enters into it
Is the god's affair; and whatever the handbooks say,
You can neither command his presence nor explain it –
All you can do is to make it possible.
If the sacrifice catches fire of its own accord
On the altar, well and good. But do not
Flatter yourself that discipline and devotion
Have wrought the miracle: they have only allowed it.

So luck is all I can wish you, or need wish you.
And every time you prepare to lay yourself
On the altar and offer again what you have to offer,
Remember, my son,
Those words – patience, joy, disinterestedness.

THE HOUSE WHERE I WAS BORN

An elegant, shabby, white-washed house
With a slate roof. Two rows
Of tall sash windows. Below the porch, at the foot of
The steps, my father, posed
In his pony trap and round clerical hat.
This is all the photograph shows.

No one is left alive to tell me
In which of those rooms I was born,
Or what my mother could see, looking out one April
Morning, her agony done,
Or if there were pigeons to answer my cooings
From that tree to the left of the lawn.

Elegant house, how well you speak
For the one who fathered me there,
With your sanguine face, your moody provincial charm,

And that Anglo-Irish air
Of living beyond one's means to keep up
An era beyond repair.

Reticent house in the far Queen's County,*
How much you leave unsaid.
Not a ghost of a hint appears at your placid windows
That she, so youthfully wed,
Who bore me, would move elsewhere very soon
And in four years be dead.

I know that we left you before my seedling
Memory could root and twine
Within you. Perhaps that is why so often I gaze
At your picture, and try to divine
Through it the buried treasure, the lost life –
Reclaim what was yours, and mine.

I put up the curtains for them again
And light a fire in their grate:
I bring the young father and mother to lean above me,
Ignorant, loving, complete:
I ask the questions I never could ask them
Until it was too late.

CHRISTMAS EVE

Come out for a while and look from the outside in
At a room you know
As the firelight fitfully beats on the windowpane –
An old heart sinking low,
And the whispering melting kisses of the snow
Soothe time from your brow.

*Queen's County: now Co. Laois.

It is Christmastide. Does the festival promise as fairly
As ever to you? 'I feel
The numbness of one whose drifted years conceal
His original landmarks of good and ill.
For a heart weighed down by its own and the world's folly
This season has little appeal.'

But tomorrow is Christmas Day. Can it really mean
Nothing to you? 'It is hard
To see it as more than a time-worn, tinsel routine,
Or else a night incredibly starred,
Angels, oxen, a Babe – the recurrent dream
Of a Christmas card.'

You must try again. Say 'Christmas Eve'. Now, quick,
What do you see?
'I see in the firelit room a child is awake,
Mute with expectancy
For the berried day, the presents, the Christmas cake.
Is he mine? or me?'

He is you, and yours. Desiring for him tomorrow's
Feast – the crackers, the Tree, the piled
Presents – you lose your self in his yearning, and borrow
His eyes to behold
Your own young world again. Love's mystery is revealed
When the father becomes the child.

'Yet would it not make those carolling angels weep
To think how incarnate Love
Means such trivial joys to us children of unbelief?'
No. It's a miracle great enough
If through centuries, clouded and dingy, this Day can keep
Expectation alive.

LOT 96*

Lot 96: a brass-rimmed ironwork fender.
It had stood guard for years, where it used to belong,
Over the hearth of a couple who loved tenderly.
Now it will go for a song.

Night upon winter night, as she gossiped with him
Or was silent, he watched the talkative firelight send
Its reflections twittering over that burnished rim
Like a language of world without end.

Death, which unclasped their hearts, dismantled all.
The world they made is as if it had never been true –
That firelit bubble of warmth, serene, magical,
Ageless in form and hue.

Now there stands, dulled in an auction room,
This iron thing – a far too durable irony,
Reflecting never a ghost of the lives that illumed it,
No hint of the sacred fire.

This lot was part of their precious bond, almost
A property of its meaning. Here, in the litter
Washed up by death, values are re-assessed
At a nod from the highest bidder.

ON A DORSET UPLAND

The floor of the high wood all smoking with bluebells,
Sap a-flare, wildfire weed, a here-and-gone wing,
Frecklings of sunlight and flickerings of shadowleaf –
How quick, how gustily kindles the spring,
Consumes our spring!

* From 1953 to 1957 we lived at 96 Campden Hill Road, London.

Tall is the forenoon of larks forever tingling:
A vapour trail, threading the blue, frays out
Slowly to a tasselled fringe; and from horizon
To horizon amble white eternities of cloud,
Sleepwalking cloud.

Here in this niche on the face of the May morning,
Fast between vale and sky, growth and decay,
Dream with the clouds, my love, throb to the awakened
Earth who has quickened a paradise from clay,
Sweet air and clay.

Now is a chink between two deaths, two eternities.
Seed here, root here, perennially cling!
Love me today and I shall live today always!
Blossom, my goldenmost, at-long-last spring,
My long, last spring!

MOODS OF LOVE

1

The melting poles, the tongues that play at lightning,
All that gross hurricane hatched from a sigh –
These are the climax to his sure routine.
But first, a glance coins gold in the air, doves issue
From clasped hands, knots no one saw tied are tightening;
The card you chose, or were made to, wondrously
Turns up here there and anywhere like a djinn,
And borrowed time vanishes to amaze you.

Admire the 'fluence of this conjuring
As once again he runs the gamut through
Of tricks you can neither fathom nor resist,
Though well you know the old Illusionist
Employs for his whole repertoire only two
Simple properties – a rod, a ring.

Think of his transformations; thirsty babe,
Secret companion, devil, confidante,
Lapdog and sphinx – each hides that king whose orb
Is the whole earth grasped in a bare 'I want'.
Redder the rose for him, sadder the fall,
Who swells a trivial word into a portent,
Turns dust to diamond, shows the bantam tall,
The giant weak: nevertheless, most potent
When he comes back insidious and subdued
As an old jailbird begging one more chance.
Whether you trust him then, or look askance,
Or slam your door, at least don't act the prude:
He's what you've made of him: plausible, lewd
Or tough, he's your flesh – was a pure child once.

3

'Oh shelter me from the invisible rain
Corrodes my flesh piecemeal! Oh take me in –
I'll be your god, your man, your mannikin!'
Cry the gaunt lecher and the ignorant swain.

Dipped in eternity now, they find nowhere
A flaw in the magic circle of their embracing:
Two are reborn as one: where all is passing
They dream a now for ever and set fair.

Reborn! The very word is like a bell.
From the warm trance, the virgin arms awoken,
Each turns to his sole self. Out of the shell
They step, unchanged. Only a spell is broken.

Though there's no cure, no making whole, no fusion,
Live while you can the merciful illusion.

4

See, at a turn of her wrist, paradise open;
Dote, lover, upon a turquoise vein;
Feel how the blood flowers and the nerves go lilting
Like butterflies through an immortal blue.
This is creation morning. What could happen
But miracles here? The god you entertain,
The pure legend you breathe, no desert silting
Over your garden ever makes untrue.

New-seen, first-named, your own to hurt and heal,
This commonplace of skin, bone, habit, sense
Is now a place that never was before.
Lose and possess yourself therein: adore
The ideal clay, the carnal innocence.
Where all's miraculous, all is most real.

5

Inert, blanched, naked, at the gale's last gasp
Out of their drowning bliss flung high and dry
Above the undertow, the breakers' rasp,
With shells and weed and shining wrack they lie.
Or, as an isle asleep with its reflection
Upon the absolute calm, each answers each
In the twin trance of an unflawed affection
That shows the substance clear, the dream in reach.
By one arched, hollowing, toppling wave uptossed
Together on the gentle dunes, they know
A world more lucid for lust's afterglow,
Where, fondly separate, blind passion fused
To a reflective glass, each holds in trust
The other's peace, and finds his real self so.

6

The dance, the plumage, all that flaunting day
Of blood's clairvoyance and enchanter's wit
Making trite things unique – you reckon it
Tells more than brute necessity at play?

Unwise. Another tedious, piteous woman
Was Helen, got by heart. Can you adore
The human animal's ecstasy, yet ignore
The ground and primitive logic of being human? –

Deplore that closest viewed is clearliest changing,
And least enduring is the most enthralling?
That love breeds habit, habit brings estranging?
That highest flown means most abysmal falling?

When the flushed hour goes down, what residue
From its broad-glittering flood remains to you?

7

Shells, weed, discoloured wrack – a spring tide's litter
Dully recalling its lost element,
And one you live with, quarrelsome or complying,
Are all that's left of Aphrodite's birth.
Gone is the power she gave you to delight her,
The period of grace, so quickly spent,
When the day's walk was a white dream of flying,
Earth a far cry, she a sufficient earth.

Whether long use has now choked your desire
With its own clinker, or, abruptly parted
At love's high noon, incredulous you have stood
Suffering her absence like a loss of blood
Week after week, still, by the god deserted,
You worship relics of a sacred fire.

8

Beware! Such idolizing can divorce
Body and mind: the foam-bright fiction drains
Purpose away and sings you from your course.
Better a brutal twitching of the reins
And off, than this devouring pious whore
Who in a soft regret will twine you fast

Where thigh-bones mope along the tainted shore
And crazed beachcombers pick over their past.
Love is the venturing on: think – as you fare
Among strange islands, each a phantasy
Of home, giving your strength to what must be
Found and new-found through doubt, mirage, despair –
Weaving, unweaving her true self somewhere
Deep in your heart grows a Penelope.

9

If love means exploration – the divine
Growth of a new discoverer first conceived
In flesh, only the stranger can be loved:
Familiar loving grooves its own decline.

If change alone is true – the ever-shifting
Base of each real or illusive show,
Inconstancy's a law: the you that now
Loves her, to otherness is blindly drifting.

But chance and fretting time and your love change her
Subtly from year to year, from known to new:
So she will always be the elusive stranger,
If you can hold her present self in view.

Find here, in constant change, faithful perceiving,
The paradox and mode of all true loving.

from THE GATE

THE GATE

For Trekkie

In the foreground, clots of cream-white flowers (meadowsweet?
Guelder? Cow parsley?): a patch of green: then a gate
Dividing the green from a brown field; and beyond,
By steps of mustard and sainfoin-pink, the distance
Climbs right-handed away
Up to an olive hilltop and the sky.

The gate it is, dead-centre, ghost-amethyst-hued,
Fastens the whole together like a brooch.
It is all arranged, all there, for the gate's sake
Or for what may come through the gate. But those white flowers,
Craning their necks, putting their heads together,
Like a crowd that holds itself back from surging forward,
Have their own point of balance – poised, it seems,
On the airy brink of whatever it is they await.

And I, gazing over their heads from outside the picture,
Question what we are waiting for: not summer –
Summer is here in charlock, grass and sainfoin.
A human event? – but there's no path to the gate,
Nor does it look as if it was meant to open.
The ghost of one who often came this way
When there was a path? I do not know. But I think,
If I could go deep into the heart of the picture

From the flowers' point of view, all I would ask is
Not that the gate should open, but that it should
Stay there, holding the coloured folds together.
We expect nothing (the flowers might add), we only
Await: this pure awaiting –
It is the kind of worship we are taught.

THE NEWBORN

(D. M. B.: April 29th, 1957)*

This mannikin who just now
Broke prison and stepped free
Into his own identity –
Hand, foot and brow
A finished work, a breathing miniature –
Was still, one night ago,
A hope, a dread, a mere shape we
Had lived with, only sure
Something would grow
Out of its coiled nine-month nonentity.

Heaved hither on quickening throes,
Tossed up on earth today,
He sprawls limp as a castaway
And nothing knows
Beside the warm sleep of his origin.
Soon lips and hands shall grope
To try the world; this speck of clay
And spirit shall begin
To feed on hope,
To learn how truth blows cold and loves betray.

Now like a blank sheet
His lineaments appear;
But there's invisible writing here
Which the day's heat
Will show: legends older than language, glum
Histories of the tribe,
Directives from his near and dear –
Charms, curses, rules of thumb –
He will transcribe
In his own blood to write upon an heir.

* Our son: Daniel Michael Blake Day Lewis.

This morsel of man I've held –
What potency it has,
Though strengthless still and naked as
A nut unshelled!
Every newborn seems a reviving seed
Or metaphor of the divine,
Charged with the huge, weak power of grass
To split rock. How we need
Any least sign
That our stone age can break, our winter pass!

Welcome to earth, my child!
Joybells of blossom swing,
Lambs and lovers have their fling,
The streets run wild
With April airs and rumours of the sun.
We time-worn folk renew
Ourselves at your enchanted spring,
As though mankind's begun
Again in you.
This is your birthday and our thanksgiving.

SHEEPDOG TRIALS IN HYDE PARK

For Robert Frost

A shepherd stands at one end of the arena.
Five sheep are unpenned at the other. His dog runs out
In a curve to behind them, fetches them straight to the shepherd,
Then drives the flock round a triangular course
Through a couple of gates and back to his master; two
Must be sorted there from the flock, then all five penned.
Gathering, driving away, shedding and penning
Are the plain words for the miraculous game.

An abstract game. What can the sheepdog make of such
Simplified terrain? – no hills, dales, bogs, walls, tracks,
Only a quarter-mile plain of grass, dumb crowds
Like crowds on hoardings around it, and behind them
Traffic or mounds of lovers and children playing.
Well, the dog is no landscape-fancier; his whole concern
Is with his master's whistle, and of course
With the flock – sheep are sheep anywhere for him.

The sheep are the chanciest element. Why, for instance,
Go through this gate when there's on either side of it
No wall or hedge but huge and viable space?
Why not eat the grass instead of being pushed around it?
Like blobs of quicksilver on a tilting board
The flock erratically runs, dithers, breaks up,
Is reassembled: their ruling idea is the dog;
And behind the dog, though they know it not yet, is a shepherd.

The shepherd knows that time is of the essence
But haste calamitous. Between dog and sheep
There is always an ideal distance, a perfect angle;
But these are constantly varying, so the man
Should anticipate each move through the dog, his medium.
The shepherd is the brain behind the dog's brain,
But his control of dog, like dog's of sheep,
Is never absolute – that's the beauty of it.

For beautiful it is. The guided missiles,
The black-and-white angels follow each quirk and jink of
The evasive sheep, play grandmother's steps behind them,
Freeze to the ground, or leap to head off a straggler
Almost before it knows that it wants to stray,
As if radar-controlled. But they are not machines –
You can feel them feeling mastery, doubt, chagrin:
Machines don't frolic when their job is done.

What's needfully done in the solitude of sheep-runs –
Those tough, real tasks – becomes this stylized game,
A demonstration of intuitive wit
Kept natural by the saving grace of error.
To lift, to fetch, to drive, to shed, to pen
Are acts I recognize, with all they mean
Of shepherding the unruly, for a kind of
Controlled woolgathering is my work too.

CIRCUS LION

Lumbering haunches, pussyfoot tread, a pride of
Lions under the arcs
Walk in, leap up, sit pedestalled there and glum
As a row of Dickensian clerks.

Their eyes are slag. Only a muscle flickering,
A bored, theatrical roar
Witness now to the furnaces that drove them
Exultant along the spoor.

In preyward, elastic leap they are sent through paper
Hoops at another's will
And a whip's crack: afterwards, in their cages,
They tear the provided kill.

Caught young, can this public animal ever dream of
Stars, distances and thunders?
Does he twitch in sleep for ticks, dried water-holes,
Rogue elephants, or hunters?

Sawdust, not burning desert, is the ground
Of his to-fro, to-fro pacing,
Barred with the zebra shadows that imply
Sun's free wheel, man's coercing.

See this abdicated beast, once king
Of them all, nibble his claws:
Not anger enough left – no, nor despair –
To break his teeth on the bars.

GETTING WARM – GETTING COLD

For Tamasin*

We hid it behind the yellow cushion.
'There's a present for you,' we called,
'Come in and look for it.' So she prowled
About the suddenly mysterious room –
'Getting warm,' she heard, 'getting cold.'

She moved in a dream of discovery, searching
Table and shelf and floor –
As if to prolong the dream, everywhere
But behind that cushion. Her invisible present
Was what she lived in there.

Would she never find it? Willing her on,
We cried, 'you're cold, you're warm,
You're burning hot,' and the little room
Was enlarged to a whole Ali Baba's cave
By her eyes' responsive flame.

May she keep this sense of the hidden thing,
The somewhere joy that enthralled her,
When she's uncountable presents older –
Small room left for marvels, and none to say
'You are warmer, now you are colder.'

* Our daughter: Tamasin Day Lewis.

WALKING AWAY

For Sean*

It is eighteen years ago, almost to the day –
A sunny day with the leaves just turning,
The touch-lines new-ruled – since I watched you play
Your first game of football, then, like a satellite
Wrenched from its orbit, go drifting away

Behind a scatter of boys. I can see
You walking away from me towards the school
With the pathos of a half-fledged thing set free
Into a wilderness, the gait of one
Who finds no path where the path should be.

That hesitant figure, eddying away
Like a winged seed loosened from its parent stem,
Has something I never quite grasp to convey
About nature's give-and-take – the small, the scorching
Ordeals which fire one's irresolute clay.

I have had worse partings, but none that so
Gnaws at my mind still. Perhaps it is roughly
Saying what God alone could perfectly show –
How selfhood begins with a walking away,
And love is proved in the letting go.

THIS YOUNG GIRL†

This young girl, whose secret life
Vagues her eyes to the reflective, lucent
Look of the sky topping a distant
Down beyond which, invisible, lies the sea –

* CDL's first-born son.
† Written after a visit to Janet and Reynolds Stone and their four children at the Old
Rectory, Litton Cheney, Dorset.

What does she mark, to remember, of the close things
That pearl-calm gaze now shines upon? . . .
Her mother, opening a parasol,
Drifts over the hailed-with-daisies lawn:

Head full of designs, her father
Is pinned to a drawing board: two brothers settle
For cool jazz in the barn: a little
Sister decides to become Queen Pocahontas.

Or is it the skyline viewed from her attic window
Intimating the sea, the sea
Which far off waits? or the water garden
Fluent with leaves and rivulets near by,

That will be her memory's leitmotif?
All seems acceptable – an old house sweetened
By wood-ash, a whole family seasoned
In dear pursuits and country gentleness.

But her eyes elude, this summer's day. Far, far
Ahead or deep within they peer,
Beyond those customary things
Towards some Golden Age, that is now, is here.

AN EPISODE

So then he walled her up alive
(It seemed that her betrayal must deserve
What his own agony felt like – the slow choking
Of breath and pore in a close grave)
And waited. There was no cry from her, no knocking.

– Waited for pain to end, with her
Who had been his love and any comer's whore.
Soft-spoken dreams revealed how he was wanting
The victim to turn comforter –
A chastened ghost, an unreproachful haunting.

Presently the blank wall grew eyes
That hunted him from every covert ease
And thickset pain. He felt as if heart were searching
For heart. He saw in those whitewashed eyes
A look neither forgiving nor beseeching.

His bloody fingers tore at the wall,
Demolishing what could never salve nor seal
Its crime, but found in the nook where he had placed her
No twisted limbs, no trace at all.
His heart lay there – a mess of stone and plaster.

AN UPLAND FIELD*

By a windrowed field she made me stop.
'I love it – finding you one of these,'
She said; and I watched her tenderly stoop
Towards a sprig of shy heartsease
Among the ruined crop.

'Oh but look, it is everywhere!'
Stubble and flint and sodden tresses
Of hay were a prospect of despair:
But a myriad infant heartsease faces
Pensively eyed us there.

* Dorset – near Plush.

165

Long enough had I found that flower
Little more common than what it is named for –
A chance-come solace amid earth's sour
Failures, a minute joy that bloomed for
Its brief, precocious hour.

No marvel that she, who gives me peace
Wherein my shortening days redouble
Their yield, could magically produce
From all that harshness of flint and stubble
Whole acres of heartsease.

THE DISABUSED

(a Dramatic Monologue)

Eleven o'clock. My house creaks and settles,
Feeling the dry-rot in its old bones. Well,
It will see me out; and after that, who cares?
More than a house is perishing – civilization,
For all I know; and Helen's marriage, she tells me,
Breaking up – a mishap she seems to confuse
With the end of the world, poor girl. 'You are so calm,
'You amaze me, father,' she said: 'I feel I cannot
'Keep my head above water any longer.'
Now she has taken her tragedy to bed.
But what storms first! – this indelicate need of woman
To have emotion – hers, his, anyone's – exposed
Like bleeding lumps of meat on a butcher's counter
And poke at it with insensitive, finicky fingers!
'Helen,' I might have said, 'if I am calm
'It is because I have spent most of a lifetime
'Learning to live with myself, which is the hardest
'Marriage of all.' But to say this would only
Have underlined her notion that I had somehow
Failed her. The way she spoke about my calmness

Was to reproach me, of course, for having failed –
Not in recognizing what she suffers,
But in refusing to be infected by it:
For that's what women want – that we vibrate
To their disturbance, visibly respond –
Tears, smiles, exasperation, pity, rage,
Any response will satisfy them, for so
Their weakness sees its power. She'll never grasp
How a man grows strong by silently outstaring
His brute infirmity. 'Helen,' I all but told her,
'Tomorrow is the fortieth anniversary
'Of the day I let my brother drown.'
                                        Not 'saw'
Or 'watched' – you notice, Tom – but 'let'. I never
Permit myself the soft and venial option . . .
It's the first morning of a summer holiday
After the War. You are just demobbed, and I,
Three years younger, finished with school. We run
Along the cliff path – harebell, scabious, rampion,
Sunlight and dew on the grass – and we are running
Back into the boyhood of our world.
You, always the leader, stand at the waves' edge
Undressed, before I have scrambled down the steep path
Among those yellow poppies to the beach.
Then, like a new slide thrown on the screen, with a click
The picture is different – I on the shingle, you
Thirty yards out suddenly thrashing the calm sea
To foam, as if you had been harpooned. This happens
So quickly, and yet your dying seems to go on
For ever. You struggle silently, your eyes
Howling for help. And I, a feeble swimmer,
Must let you drown or flounder out and let you
Drag me under.
                        But there was no choice, really:
Fear, like an automatic governor,
Shut off the power in my limbs, held me down
So hard that a flint dug my bare sole open

(I have the stigma now). The cove contained
My tiny shouts. My eyes searched everywhere –
Foreshore and cliff and heaven – at first for help,
But soon to make sure there was no witness of
Your dying and my living, or perhaps
Most of all to avoid your whitening stare.
No one in sight; and at last the sea's face too
Was empy. Now I could look. Along the horizon,
Slow as a minute hand, there faintly moved
A little ship, a model of indifference.
So it went.
                              You have omitted one thing.
No, Tom, I was coming to that. I lay down
In the shallows to saturate my clothes.
('What presence of mind,' you say? A coward soon
Learns circumspection.) So, when I got home
Crying, limping, dripping with brine, father
In his crammed anguish still found room to praise me,
Console and praise me for having done my best.

There's this to be said for growing old – one loses
The itch for wholeness, the need to justify
One's maimed condition. I have lived all these years
A leper beneath the skin, scrupulous always
To keep away from where I could spread contagion.
No one has guessed my secret. I had to learn
Good and early the know-how of consuming
My own waste products: I at least have never
Contaminated soil or river. Why,
Why then, though I have played the man in facing
My worst, and cauterized the ugly wound,
Does that original morning by the sea
Still irk me like a lovers' tryst unkept –
Not with remorse or tragedy curses – no,
With the nostalgic sweetness of some vision
All but made flesh, then vanishing, which drains
Colour and pith from the whole aftertime?

168

I lost a brother
                    Only a brother?
                                        Tom,
Do you mean self-respect? We have had this out
A hundred times. You know I have regained it,
Stiffening my heart against its primal fault.
'There was the fault,' you say? What? Do you blame
The wound for the scar-tissue, or a bombed site
For growing willowherb? It is nature's way.
You who gulped the sea and are dead, why do you
Keep swimming back with these cast-off things in your mouth
Like an imbecile dog?
                    The vision. The sweet vision.
Recapture. A last chance.
                                        This is beyond me!
Last chance of what? Is it your elder-brotherly
Pleasure to keep me wallowing in that sour
Humiliation? You can teach me nothing
About the anatomy of fear – I've made it
A life-long study, through self-vivisection:
And if I did use local anaesthetics
To deaden the area, better a witness than
A victim to the science of self-knowledge.
Relentlessly I have tracked each twist and shuffle,
Face-saving mask, false candour, truth-trimmed fraud.
All stratagems of bluster and evasion –
Traced them back along the quivering nerves
To that soft monster throned in my being's chasm,
Till I was armed in and against the infirmity.
Self-knowledge. I tell you, Tom, we do not solve
Human problems with tears and kisses: each,
Like one of my engineering jobs, demands
Calculation of stresses and resistance.
If the material's faulty
                    Poor father,
Must you fail me then?

169

Helen! You too?
How can you put such nonsense into my head?
I said I would do all that I can to help you,
See the lawyers, have you and the children here –
Practical things. 'Consider this your home now,'
I said. A storm of animal sobbing then,
As though I had struck her. Good Lord, does she expect me
To interview Robert and make him return to her?
If only her mother was alive! – such scenes
Afflict me with a rigor of repulsion.
Curious, that: how near we come to loathing
Those whose demands, however unreasonable,
We fail to meet – yes, impotence humiliates,
Not in bed only.
                              Father, do you love me?
Love you? Of course I do. You are my daughter.
She used to remind me, as a child, of Tom –
The same blue, mocking, meditative gaze . . .
Azure eye of the sea, wakeful, dangerous.
Between the sea's eye and the yellow poppies
A vision to recapture? . . . I perceive
One drowning, one not drowning, that is all.
No, Tom, let us stick to facts: the relevant fact is
That it was you, not I, who died that day.
Well, do you deny it? Do you deny it? Speak to me!
You cannot. You are dead, I am alive.
Let sleeping visions lie. How could he think
I should breach the dyke I have been all these years
Building and reinforcing? Ah, I see it –
Trying to lure me out of my depth – the same
As Helen an hour ago, – 'Come, father, jump
Into the boiling sea of my emotions
And let us choke together.'
                              If you love me,
Father, stretch out a hand.
                              If stretching out
My hand could rescue, I would do it: but

Father, if you can love, stretch out your hand.
Well, gestures are the easiest way to humour
A woman. So why not reach out my hand,
As it might be over the breakfast table tomorrow,
Reach out this hand to Helen, so. Reach out –
Christ, I cannot! Won't move, it won't move!
What's this? A seizure, a stroke? Move, damn you!
Dying? No! No! I cannot die yet.
Dreaming. A bad dream. Overwork. Of course.
Jackson's arm caught in the hydraulic press.
Man with a withered arm, in the Bible: atrophy –
No, that's gradual. Cramp. Tom died of it.
But there's no agony, not a twinge – God!
Let me feel something! I have gone dead, quite dead:
All power cut off . . . If I could analyse
My feelings, I should – cogito, ergo sum –
But there's no feeling, only an Arctic night
Of numb, eternal fear, death's null forever.
Dead, then? How long? How long? Eleven-fifteen,
The clock says. My nightcap still on the table;
And there's my hand, reaching out to take it.
Reaching! Alive! . .
                              My God, I needed that.
What a grotesque hallucination! Really,
I could have sworn my arm was paralysed
For a few moments. If I were superstitious,
I'd say it was a sign from heaven – yes, Tom,
It rather proves my point – a sign that I
Was right not to embroil myself in Helen's
Hysterical maelstrom. What she needs from me
Is rational guidance, realism, detachment,
Not facile gestures of pure self-indulgence.
You and your 'vision', Tom! No, I'm not buying it.
One delusion is quite enough . . . I'd better
Ring MacIntyre in the morning, and arrange
For him to give me a thorough overhaul.

171

from THE ROOM

ON NOT SAYING EVERYTHING

This tree outside my window here,
Naked, umbrageous, fresh or sere,
Has neither chance nor will to be
Anything but a linden tree,
Even if its branches grew to span
The continent; for nature's plan
Insists that infinite extension
Shall create no new dimension.
From the first snuggling of the seed
In earth, a branchy form's decreed.

Unwritten poems loom as if
They'd cover the whole of earthly life.
But each one, growing, learns to trim its
Impulse and meaning to the limits
Roughed out by me, then modified
In its own truth's expanding light.
A poem, settling to its form,
Finds there's no jailer, but a norm
Of conduct, and a fitting sphere
Which stops it wandering everywhere.

As for you, my love, it's harder,
Though neither prisoner nor warder,
Not to desire you both: for love
Illudes us we can lightly move
Into a new dimension, where
The bounds of being disappear
And we make one impassioned cell.
So wanting to be all in all
Each for each, a man and woman
Defy the limits of what's human.

175

Your glancing eye, your animal tongue,
Your hands that flew to mine and clung
Like birds on bough, with innocence
Masking those young experiments
Of flesh, persuaded me that nature
Formed us each other's god and creature.
Play out then, as it should be played,
The sweet illusion that has made
An eldorado of your hair
And our love an everywhere.

But when we cease to play explorers
And become settlers, clear before us
Lies the next need – to re-define
The boundary between yours and mine;
Else, one stays prisoner, one goes free.
Each to his own identity
Grown back, shall prove our love's expression
Purer for this limitation.
Love's essence, like a poem's, shall spring
From the not saying everything.

DERELICT

*For A. D. Peters**

The soil, flinty at best, grew sour. Its yield
Receding left the old farm high and dry
On a ledge of the hills. Disused, the rutted field-
Track fades, like the sound of footsteps, into a sigh
For any feet to approach this padlocked door.
The walls are stained and cracked, the roof's all rafter.
We have come where silence opens to devour

* A. D. Peters was CDL's literary agent and close friend for forty-six years of his writing life.

Owl-cry, wind-cry, all human memories . . . After
So many working life-times a farm settles
For leisure, and in the tenth of a life-time goes
To seed . . . A harrow rusts among harsh nettles.
She who in love or protest grew that rose
Beneath her window, left nothing else behind
But a mangle in the wash-house. The rose now
Looks mostly thorn and sucker; the window's blind
With cobwebs. Dilapidated! – even the low
Front wall is ragged: neighbours have filched its stone
To build their pigsties, maybe; but what neighbours? –
Never did a farm stand more alone.
Was it the loneliness, then, and not their labour's
Poor yield that drove them out? A farmer's used
To the silence of things growing, weather breeding.
More solitude, more acres. He'd be amused
To hear it's human company he was needing.
With a wife to bake, wash, mend, to nag or share
The after-supper silence, children to swing
From those rheumatic apple trees; and where
The docks run wild, his chained-up mongrel barking
If anyone climbed a mile off on the hill.
He'd not abandon cheerfully a place
In which he'd sunk his capital of skill
And sweat. But if earth dies on you, it's no disgrace
To pull up roots . . . Now, all that was the farm's –
The same demands of seasons, the plain grit
And homely triumph – deepens and informs
The silence you can hear. Reverence it.

FISHGUARD TO ROSSLARE

From all my childhood voyages back to Ireland
Only two things remembered: gulls afloat
Off Fishguard quay, littering a patch of radiance
Shed by the midnight boat.

And at dawn a low, dun coast shaping to meet me,
An oyster sky opening above Rosslare . . .
I rub the sleep from my eyes. Gulls pace the moving
Mast-head. We're almost there.

Gulls white as a dream on the pitch of Fishguard harbour,
Paper cut-outs, birds on a lacquered screen;
The low coastline and the pearl sky of Ireland;
A long sleep in between.

A sleep between two waking dreams – the haven,
The landfall – is how it appears now. The child's eye,
Unpuzzled, saw plain facts: I catch a glint from
The darkness they're haunted by.

THE DAM

It mounted up behind his cowardice
And self-regard. Fearing she would expose
His leper tissue of half-truths and lies
When, hurt, she probed at him, he tried to gloze
That fear as patience with her sick mistrust
Of him: he could not answer her appeal,
Nor recognize how his was the accursed
Patience of flesh that can no longer feel . . .
Love had once mounted up behind his fear
Of being exposed in love's whole helplessness,
And broke it down, and carried him to her
On the pure, toppling rage for nakedness . . .
A spate of her reproaches. The dam broke.
In deluging anger his self-hatred spoke.

ELEGY FOR A WOMAN UNKNOWN

(F. P.) *

I

At her charmed height of summer –
Prospects, children rosy,
In the heart's changeful music
Discords near resolved –
Her own flesh turned upon her:
The gross feeder slowly
Settled to consume her.

Pain speaks, bearing witness
Of rank cells that spawn
To bring their temple down.
Against such inmost treachery
Futile our protesting:
The body creates its own
Justice and unjustness.

Three times flesh was lopped,
As trees to make a firebreak.
(In their natural flowering
Beautiful the trees.)
Three times her enemy leapt
The gap. Three years of dying
Before the heart stopped.

---

* In 1961, Dr Michael Peters came to see CDL at Chatto and Windus, bringing a sheaf of his wife's poems: she had recently died of cancer. C prayed that they would be good enough to publish. They weren't. When we were voyaging in Greece that summer, he started to write a poem on the island of Delos at sunset, as he sat, head in hands, gazing at the stone lions. He tried to make it a poem she would like to have written.

Upon the shrinking islands
Of flesh and hope, among
Bitter waves that plunged,
Withdrew to lunge yet deeper,
Patient, unreconciled,
She wrote poems and flung them
To the approaching silence.

Upon the stretching hours
Crucified alone,
She grew white as a stone
Image of endurance;
Soft only to the cares
Of loved ones – all concern
For lives that would soon lack hers.

Dying, did she pass through
Despair to the absolute
Self-possession – the lightness
Of knowing a world indifferent
To all we suffer and do,
Shedding the clung-to load
Of habit, illusion, duty?

You who watched, phase by phase,
Her going whose life was meshed
With yours in grief and passion,
Remember now the unspoken,
Unyielding word she says –
How, in ruinous flesh,
Heroic the heart can blaze.

II
Island of stone and silence. A rough ridge
Chastens the innocent azure. Lizards hang
Like their own shadows crucified on stone
(But the heart palpitates, the ruins itch

180

With memories amid the sunburnt grass). Here sang
Apollo's choir, the sea their unloosed zone.
Island of stillness and white stone.

Marble and stone – the ground-plan is suggested
By low walls, plinths, lopped columns of stoa, streets
Clotted with flowers dead in June, where stood
The holy place. At dusk they are invested
With Apollonian calm and a ghost of his zenith heats.
But now there are no temples and no god:
Vacantly stone and marble brood,

And silence – not the silence after music,
But the silence of no more music. A breeze twitches
The grass like a whisper of snakes; and swallows there are,
Cicadas, frogs in the cistern. But elusive
Their chorusing – thin threads of utterance, vanishing stitches
Upon the gape of silence, whose deep core
Is the stone lions' soundless roar.

Lions of Delos, roaring in abstract rage
Below the god's hill, near his lake of swans!
Tense haunches, rooted paws set in defiance
Of time and all intruders, each grave image
Was sentinel and countersign of deity once.
Now they have nothing to keep but the pure silence.
Crude as a schoolchild's sketch of lions

They hold a rhythmic truth, a streamlined pose.
Weathered by sea-winds into beasts of the sea,
Fluent from far, unflawed; but the jaws are toothless,
Granulated by time the skin, seen close,
And limbs disjointed. Nevertheless, what majesty
Their bearing shows – how well they bear these ruthless
Erosions of their primitive truth!

Thyme and salt on my tongue, I commune with
Those archetypes of patience, and with them praise
What in each frantic age can most incline
To reverence; accept from them perfection's myth –
One who warms, clarifies, inspires, and flays.
Sweetness he gives but also, being divine,
Dry bitterness of salt and thyme.

The setting sun has turned Apollo's hill
To darker honey. Boulders and burnt grass.
A lyre-thin wind. A landscape monochrome.
Birds, lizards, lion shapes are all stone-still.
Ruins and mysteries in the favouring dusk amass,
While I reach out through silence and through stone
To her whose sun has set, the unknown.

III

We did not choose to voyage.
Over the ship's course we had little say,
And less over the ship. Tackle
Fraying; a little seamanly skill picked up on our way;
Cargo, that sooner or later we should
Jettison to keep afloat for one more day.
But to have missed the voyage –

That would be worse than the gales, inglorious calms,
Hard tack and quarrels below . . .
Ship's bells, punctual as hunger; dawdling stars;
Duties – to scrub the deck, to stow
Provisions, break out a sail: if crisis found us of one mind,
It was routine that made us so,
And hailed each landfall like a first-born son.

Figure to yourself the moment
When, after weeks of the crowding emptiness of sea
(Though no two waves are the same to an expert
Helmsman's eye), the wind bears tenderly

From an island still invisible
The smell of earth – of thyme, grass, olive trees:
Fragrance of a woman lost, returning.

And you open the bay, like an oyster, but sure there'll be
A pearl inside; and rowing ashore,
Are received like gods. They shake down mulberries into
Your lap, bring goat's cheese, pour
Fresh water for you, and wine. Love too is given.
It's for the voyaging that you store
Such memories; yet each island seems your abiding-place.

. . . For the voyaging, I say:
And not to relieve its hardships, but to merge
Into its element. Bays we knew
Where still, clear water dreamed like a demiurge
And we were part of his fathomless dream;
Times, we went free and frisking with dolphins through the surge
Upon our weather bow.

Those were our best hours – the mind disconnected
From pulsing Time, and purified
Of accidents: those, and licking the salt-stiff lips,
The rope-seared palms, happy to ride
With sea-room after days of clawing from off a lee shore,
After a storm had died.
Oh, we had much to thank Poseidon for.

Whither or why we voyaged,
Who knows? . . . A worst storm blew. I was afraid.
The ship broke up. I swam till I
Could swim no more. My love and memories are laid
In the unrevealing deep . . . But tell them
They need not pity me. Tell them I was glad
Not to have missed the voyage.

MY MOTHER'S SISTER*

I see her against the pearl sky of Dublin
Before the turn of the century, a young woman
With all those brothers and sisters, green eyes, hair
She could sit on; for high life, a meandering sermon

(Church of Ireland) each Sunday, window-shopping
In Dawson Street, picnics at Killiney and Howth . . .
To know so little about the growing of one
Who was angel and maid-of-all-work to my growth!

– Who, her sister dying, took on the four-year
Child, and the chance that now she would never make
A child of her own; who, mothering me, flowered in
The clover-soft authority of the meek.

Who, exiled, gossiping home chat from abroad
In roundhand letters to a drift of relations –
Squires', Goldsmiths, Overends, Williams' – sang the songs
Of Zion in a strange land. Hers the patience

Of one who made no claims, but simply loved
Because that was her nature, and loving so
Asked no more than to be repaid in kind.
If she was not a saint, I do not know

What saints are . . . Buying penny toys at Christmas
(The most a small purse could afford) to send her
Nephews and nieces, she'd never have thought the shop
Could shine for me one day in Bethlehem splendour.

Exiled again after ten years, my father
Remarrying, she faced the bitter test
Of charity – to abdicate in love's name
From love's contentful duties. A distressed

* Agnes Squires, known as 'Knos'.

184

Gentle woman housekeeping for strangers;
Later, companion to a droll recluse
Clergyman brother in rough-pastured Wexford,
She lived for all she was worth – to be of use.

She bottled plums, she visited parishioners.
A plain habit of innocence, a faith
Mildly forbearing, made her one of those
Who, we were promised, shall inherit the earth.

. . . Now, sunk in one small room of a Rathmines
Old people's home, helpless, beyond speech
Or movement, yearly deeper she declines
To imbecility – my last link with childhood.

The battery's almost done: yet if I press
The button hard – some private joke in boyhood
I teased her with – there comes upon her face
A glowing of the old, enchanted smile.

So, still alive, she rots. A heart of granite
Would melt at this unmeaning sequel. Lord,
How can this be justified, how can it
Be justified?

THIS LOAFER

In a sun-crazed orchard
Busy with blossomings
This loafer, unaware of
What toil or weather brings,
Lumpish sleeps – a chrysalis
Waiting, no doubt, for wings.

185

And when he does get active,
It's not for business – no
Bee-lines to thyme or heather,
No earnest to-and-fro
Of thrushes: pure caprice tells him
Where and how to go.

All he can ever do
Is to be entrancing,
So that a child may think,
Upon a chalk-blue chancing,
'Today was special. I met
A piece of the sky dancing.'

from THE WHISPERING ROOTS

BALLINTUBBERT HOUSE, CO. LAOIS*

Here is the unremembered gate.
Two asses, a grey and a black,
Have ambled across from the rough lawn
As if they'd been told to greet
The revenant. Trees draw graciously back
As I follow the drive, to unveil
For this drifty wraith, composed and real
The house where he was born.

Nothing is changed from that sixty-year-old
Photograph, except
My father's young face has been brushed away.
On the steps down which he strolled
With me in his arms, the living are grouped,
And it is my son Sean
Who stands upon the dishevelled lawn
To photograph us today.

I walk through the unremembered house,
Note on the walls each stain
Of damp; then up the spacious stair
As if I would now retrace
My self to the room where it began.
Dust on fine furnishings,
A scent of wood ash – the whole house sings
With an elegiac air.

Its owner is not at home – nor I
Who have no title in it
And no drowned memories to chime
Through its hush. Can piety

* Laois: pronounced Leash. Ballintubbert House was the poet's birthplace.

Or a long-lost innocence explain it? –
By what prodigious spell,
Sad elegant house, you have made me feel
A ghost before my time?

KILMAINHAM JAIL: EASTER SUNDAY, 1966

Sunbursts over this execution yard
    Mitigate high, harsh walls. A lowly
Black cross marks the deaths we are here to honour,
    Relieved by an Easter lily.
Wearing the nineteen-sixteen medal, a few
    Veterans and white-haired women recall
The Post Office, Clanwilliam House, the College of Surgeons,
    Jacob's factory – all
Those desperate strongholds caught in a crossfire
    Between the English guns
And Dublin's withering incredulity.
    Against the wall where once
Connolly, strapped to a chair, was shot, a platform
    Holds movie cameras. They sight
On the guard of honour beneath the tricolor,
    An officer with a horseman's light
And quiet hands, and now the old President
    Who, soldierly still in bearing,
Steps out to lay a wreath under the plaque.
    As then, no grandiose words, no cheering –
Only a pause in the splatter of Dublin talk,
    A whisper of phantom volleys.

How could they know, those men in the sunless cells,
What would flower from their blood and England's follies?
Their dreams, coming full circle, had punctured upon
The violence that gave them breath and cut them loose.
They bargained on death: death came to keep the bargain.
Pious postcards of men dying in spruce

Green uniforms, angels beckoning them aloft,
Only cheapen their cause. Today they are hailed
As martyrs; but then they bore the ridiculed shame of
Mountebanks in a tragedy which has failed.
And they were neither the one nor the other – simply
Devoted men who, though the odds were stacked
Against them, believed their country's age-old plight
And the moment gave no option but to act.
Now the leaders, each in his sweating cell,
The future a blind wall and the unwinking
Eyes of firing-squad rifles, pass their time
In letters home, in prayer. Maybe they are thinking
Of Mount Street, the blazing rooftops, the Post Office,
Wrapping that glory round them against the cold
Shadow of death. Who knows the pull and recoil of
A doomed heart?

          They are gone as a tale that is told,
The fourteen men. Let them be more than a legend:
Ghost-voices of Kilmainham, claim your due –
This is not yet the Ireland we fought for.
You living, make our Easter dreams come true.

HAREBELLS OVER MANNIN BAY

Half moon of moon-pale sand.
Sea stirs in midnight blue.
Looking across to the Twelve Pins
The singular harebells stand.

The sky's all azure. Eye
To eye with them upon
Cropped grass, I note the harebells give
Faint echoes of the sky.

For such a Lilliput host
To pit their colours against
Peacock of sea and mountain seems
Impertinence at least.

These summer commonplaces,
Seen close enough, confound
A league of brilliant waves, and dance
On the grave mountain faces.

Harebells, keep your arresting
Pose by the strand. I like
These gestures of the ephemeral
Against the everlasting.

SAILING FROM CLEGGAN

Never will I forget it –
Beating out through Cleggan Bay
Towards Inishbofin, how
The shadow lay between us,
An invisible shadow
All but severing us lay
Athwart the Galway hooker.

Sea-room won, turning to port
Round Rossadillisk Point I
Slacken the sheet. Atlantic
Breeze abeam, ahead sun's eye
Opening, we skirt past reefs
And islands – Friar, Cruagh,
Orney, Eeshal, Inishturk.

Porpoises cartwheeling through
Inshore water, boom creaking,
Spray asperging; and sunlight
Transforming to a lime-green
Laughter the lipcurling of
Each morose wave as they burst
On reefs fanged for a shipwreck.

Miracle sun, dispelling
That worst shadow! Salt and sun,
Our wounds' cautery! And how,
Havened, healed, oh lightened of
The shadow, we stepped ashore
On to our recaptured love –
Never could I forget it.

GOLDSMITH OUTSIDE TRINITY

There he stands, my ancestor, back turned
On Trinity, with his friend Edmund Burke
And others of the Anglo-Irish genius –
Poet, naturalist, historian, hack.

The statue glosses over his uncouth figure,
The pock-marked face, the clownish tongue and mien:
It can say nothing of his unstaunchable charity,
But does full justice to the lack of chin.

Little esteemed by the grave and grey-faced college,
He fiddled his way through Europe, was enrolled
Among the London literates: a deserted
Village brought forth a citizen of the world.

His period and the Anglo-Irish reticence
Kept sentiment unsicklied and unfurred:
Good sense, plain style, a moralist could distinguish
Fine shades from the ignoble to the absurd.

Dublin they flew, the wild geese of Irish culture.
They fly it still: the curdled elegance,
The dirt, the cod, new hucksters, old heroics,
Look better viewed from a remoter stance.

Here from his shadow I note the buses grumbling
On to Rathmines, Stillorgan, Terenure –
Names he'd have known – and think of the arterial
Through-way between us. I would like to be sure

Long-distance genes do more than merely connect us.
But I, a provincial too, an expatriate son
Of Ireland, have nothing of that compulsive gambler,
Nothing of the inspired simpleton.

Yet, as if to an heirloom given a child and long
Unvalued, I at last have returned to him
With gratefuller recognition, get from his shadow
A wordless welcome, a sense of being brought home.

THE WHISPERING ROOTS

Roots are for holding on, and holding dear.
Mine, like a child's milk teeth, came gently away
From Ireland at the close of my second year.
Is it second childhood now – that I overhear
Them whisper across a lifetime as if from yesterday?

We have had blood enough and talk of blood,
These sixty years. Exiles are two a penny
And race a rancid word; a meaningless word
For the Anglo-Irish: a flighty cuckoo brood
Foisted on alien nests, they knew much pride and many

Falls. But still my roots go whispering on
Like rain on a soft day. Whatever lies
Beneath their cadence I could not disown:
An Irish stranger's voice, its tang and tone,
Recalls a family language I thrill to recognize.

All the melodious places only seen
On a schoolboy's map – Kinsale, Meath, Connemara:
Writers – Swift, Berkeley, Goldsmith, Sheridan:
Fighters, from Vinegar Hill to Stephen's Green:
The Sidhe*, saints, scholars, rakes of Mallow, kings of Tara: –

Were background music to my ignorant youth.
Now on a rising wind louder it swells
From the lonely hills of Laois. What can a birth-
Place mean, its features comely or uncouth,
To a long-rootless man? Yet still the place compels.

We Anglo-Irish and the memory of us
Are thinning out. Bad landlords some, some good,
But never of a land rightfully ours,
We hunted, fished, swore by our ancestors,
Till we were ripped like parasite growth from native wood.

And still the land compels me; not ancestral
Ghosts, nor regret for childhood's fabled charms,
But a rare peacefulness, consoling, festal,
As if the old religion we oppressed all
Those years folded the stray within a father's arms.

The modern age has passed this island by
And it's the peace of death her revenants find?
Harsh Dublin wit, peasant vivacity
Are here to give your shallow claims the lie.
Perhaps in such soil only the heart's long roots will bind –

* Sidhe: pronounced She.
People of the faery mound (found in Irish mythology and W. B. Yeats).

Even, transplanted, quiveringly respond
To their first parent earth. Here God is taken
For granted, time like a well-tutored hound
Brought to man's heel, and ghosting underground
Something flows to the exile from what has been forsaken.

In age, body swept on, mind crawls upstream
Toward the source; not thinking to find there
Visions or fairy gold – what old men dream
Is pure restatement of the original theme,
A sense of rootedness, a source held near and dear.

HERO AND SAINT

Sad if no one provoked us any more
    To do the improbable –
Catch a winged horse, muck out a preposterous stable,
    Or even some unsensational chore

Like becoming a saint. Those adversaries knew
    The form, to be sure: small use for one
Who after an hour of effort would throw down
    Cross, shovel or lassoo.

It gave more prestige to each prince of lies
    And his far-fetched ordeal
That an attested hero should just fail
    One little finger's breadth from the prize.

Setting for Heracles and Bellerophon
    Such tasks, they judged it a winning gamble,
Forgetting they lived in a world of myth where all
    Conclusions are foregone.

A saint knows patience alone will see him through
  Ordeals which lure, disfigure, numb:
And this (the heroes proved) can only come
  From a star kept in view.

But he forgoes the confidence, the hallowed
  Air of an antique hero:
He never will see himself but as a zero
  Following a One that gives it value.

Hero imagined himself in the constellations,
  Saint as a numbered grain of wheat.
Nowhere but in aspiring do they meet
  And discipline of patience.

He rose to a trial of wit and sinew, *he*
  To improbable heights of loving.
Both, it seems, might have been good for nothing
  Without a consummate adversary.

AT EAST COKER

At the far end of a bemusing village
Which has kept losing finding and losing itself
Along the lane, as if to exercise a pilgrim's
Faith, you see it at last. Blocked by a hill
The traffic, if there was any, must swerve aside:
Riding the hilltop, confidently saddled,
A serviceable English church.

Climb on foot now, past white lilac and
The alms-house terrace; beneath yew and cedar
Screening the red-roof blur of Yeovil; through
The peaceable aroma of June grasses,
The churchyard where old Eliots lie. Enter.

A brass on the south wall commemorates
William Dampier, son of this unhorizoned village,
Who thrice circumnavigated the globe, was
First of all Englishmen to explore
The coast of Australia . . . An exact observer
Of all things in Earth, Sea and Air. Another
Exploring man has joined his company.

In the north-west corner, sealed, his ashes are
(Remember him at a party, diffident,
Or masking his fire behind an affable mien):
Above them, today, paeonies glow like bowls of
Wine held up to the blessing light.

Where an inscription bids us pray
For the repose of the soul of T. S. Eliot, poet –
A small fee in return for the new worlds
He opened us. 'Where prayer is valid', yes,
Though mine beats vainly against death's stone front,
And all our temporal tributes only scratch
Graffiti on its monumental silence.

*   *   *

But soon obituary yields
To the real spirit, livelier and more true.
There breathes a sweetness from his honoured stone,
A discipline of long virtue,
As in that farmside chapel among fields
At Little Gidding. We rejoice for one
Whose heart a midsummer's long winter,
Though ashen-skied and droughtful, could not harden
Against the melting of midwinter spring,
When the gate into the rose garden
Opening at last permitted him to enter
Where wise man becomes child, child plays at king.
A presence, playful yet austere,

198

Courteously stooping, slips into my mind
Like a most elegant allusion clinching
An argument. Eyes attentive, lined
Forehead – 'Thus and thus runs,' he makes it clear,
'The poet's rule. No slackening, no infringing
'Must compromise it.' . . . Now, supplying
Our loss with words of comfort, his kind ghost
Says all that need be said about committedness:
Here in East Coker they have crossed
My heart again – For us there is only the trying
To learn to use words. The rest is not our business.

1970

VERS D'OCCASION

OLD VIC, 1818–1968*

Curtain up on this dear, honoured scene!
A South-bank Cinderella wears
The crown tonight of all our country's theatres.
The stage where Kean
Enthralled and Baylis wove dazzling tradition
On a shoestring, makes good the vision
Of a hundred and fifty years.

Old Vic, your roof held generations under
A magic spell. And we have known
So many incandescent nights flash past and flown
Away – no wonder,
Where the young dreamed their dreams and learned their trade,
Stars come home to celebrate
Their nursery's renown.

Here everyman once bought for a small price
Audience with Shakespeare, and still gleans
Self-knowledge from the hero's fall, the heroine's
Love-sacrifice.
This stage is all the world; in all our hearts
Rosalind smiles, Iago hates,
Lear howls, Malvolio preens.

---

* This was on a special four-page programme for the National Theatre production of *As You Like It* at the Old Vic, in the presence of Princess Marina, for the 150th Old Vic anniversary performance on 14 May 1968.

Old cockney Vic, with what strange art you bring
Us strollers into one family
That learns through discipline, patience, tears and gaiety
'The play's the thing'.
You show world theatre, old and new, today –
Man's heights and depths, and what he may
Yet crave, yet come to be.

KEEP FAITH WITH NATURE*

Animal, fish, fowl
Share with man the lease
And limits of creation.
Heron by the pool,
Tiger through the tree
Lend us images
Of action and contemplation.

Soil that gives man bread,
Flowers that feed his eye
For ages have kept him whole.
Virgin lands visited,
Forest and butterfly,
Berry, well, wave supply
The hunger of body and soul.

Now more than ever we need
True science, lest mankind
Lording it over nature's
Territories, by greed
Or thoughtlessness made blind,
To doom shall have consigned
Itself and all earth's creatures.

* Published by Midnag, Ashington, for the environment.

A SHORT DIRGE FOR ST. TRINIAN'S*

Where are the girls of yesteryear? How strange
To think they're scattered East, South, West and North –
Those pale Medusas of the Upper Fourth,
Those Marihuanas of the Moated Grange.

No more the shrieks of victims, and no more
The fiendish chuckle borne along the breeze!
Gone are the basilisk eyes, the bony knees.
Mice, and not blood, run down each corridor.

Now poison ivy twines the dorm where casks
Were broached and music mistresses were flayed,
While on the sports ground where the pupils played
The relatively harmless adder basks.

Toll for St. Trinian's, nurse of frightful girls!
St. Trinian's, mother of the far too free!
No age to come (thank God) will ever see
Such an academy as Dr. Searle's.

KEATS, 1821–1971†

Dying in Rome, mocked by the wraith
Of fame, lungs burnt out, heart consumed
With love-longing, could he have dreamed
His life had not been waste of breath?

The sanguine youth could yet despair
That poetry's great age was passed,
Her future pinched and overcast –
All said, all better said, before.

---

* A poem written on the occasion of Ronald Searle's decision to kill off St. Trinian's.
From *Souls in Torment* by Ronald Searle, 1953.
† Written for the 150th anniversary of the death of Keats, and read in Keats–Shelley
Memorial House, Rome, in February 1971, when JB and CDL gave a recital there.
My gratitude to the curator, Bathsheba Abse, for sending me a typescript of this.

After much groping a year came
When genius took his feverish hand,
Urgently pointing to the ground
Where he would strike a richest seam.

That year is gone. Today he lies
As by a losing race quite drained,
Heeds not the laurels unattained,
Comforts a sorrowing friend, and dies.

Fate took that hard death for its fee,
Then eased him into immortality.

from **POSTHUMOUS POEMS**

THE EXPULSION: MASACCIO*

They stumble in naked grief, as refugees
From a flood or pogrom, dispossessed of all
But a spray of leaf like barbed wire round the loins.
For sight, she has mere sockets gouged and charred
By nightmare, and her mouth is a bottomless pit
Of desolation. Her lord, accomplice, dupe,
Ashamed of his failure, as if he cannot face it
Covers his eyes.
              We know they left behind
A place where fruits and animals were kind
And time no enemy. But did they know their loss
As more than a child's when its habitual toys
Are confiscated for some innocent fault,
Or take the accusing cosmic voice that called
To be the same as their dear old garden god's?
The sword that pickets paradise also goads
Towards self-knowledge. More they shall come to wish
Than brutal comfort of committed flesh.
Masaccio paints us both
A childish tragedy – hunched back, bawling mouth,
And the hour when the animal knew that it must die
And with that stroke put on humanity.

* Masaccio's Frescoes in Santa Maria del Carmine, Florence, seen for the first time on a convalescent holiday 1970. The poem was published in a Festschrift for W. H. Auden's 65th birthday in 1972 in a limited edition of 500.

HELLENE: PHILHELLENE*

In memory of George Seferis and C. M. Bowra

Great poet, friend of my later days, you first
I would honour. Driven from shore to shore
Like Odysseus, everywhere you had nursed
The quivering spark of freedom, your heart's core
Loaded and lit by your country's tragedies,
Her gods and heroes. These inhabited
Your poetry with a timeless, native ease
But they moved there among the living dead
Of recent times, so myth and history
Became one medium, deeply interfused.
    I recall, in London or in Rome, you welcoming me –
Warm growl, the Greek 'my dear' – a spirit used
To catching voices from rock, tree, waves, ports,
And so always a shade preoccupied.
Hearing you were dead, I remembered your *Argonauts*,
How 'one after another the comrades died
With downcast eyes', having become reflections
And articles of the voyage: as you, whose quest is
One now with theirs. My lasting recollections –
Your grace before necessity, your passion for justice.

And you no less, dear tutor of my young days,
Lover of Greece and poetry, I mourn.
To me you seem then the exorbitant blaze
Of Aegean sun dispelling youth's forlorn
Blurred images; the lucid air; the salt

---

* First published in *Cornhill* (winter 1971–1972). Maurice Bowra had been CDL's
tutor when he read Classics at Wadham College, Oxford. We had last been reunited
with our friend George Seferis – the great Greek poet and Nobel Prizewinner – in
Rome in 1968, before the Colonels confiscated his passport. On principle, Maurice
would not now travel to Greece. It was a sacrifice. On a fiercely hot day, Cecil, himself
now mortally ill, had gone from Greenwich to Oxford to follow Maurice's coffin to the
graveside.

210

Of tonic sea on your lips. And you were one
Whom new poetic languages enthralled
(After I'd stumbled through a Greek unseen,
You'd take *The Tower* or *The Waste Land* from a shelf
And read me into strange live mysteries.)
        You taught me most by always being yourself
Those fifty years ago. For ever Greece
Remained your second country, even though
You were self-exiled latterly, touched by the same
Indignation which made that other know
Exile was not for him. Yearly your fame
Grew as administrator, scholar, wit:
But my best memory, the young man whose brilliance
Lit up my sombre skies and kept them lit,
Drawing dead poets into the ageless dance.

I miss these men of genius and good sense,
In a mad world lords of their just enclave,
My future emptier for the one's absence,
So much of my youth laid in the other's grave.
Hellene and Philhellene, both gone this year,
They leave a radiance on the heart, a taste
Of salt and honey on the tongue, a dear
Still-warm encampment in the darkening waste.

REMEMBERING CARROWNISKY*

The train window trapped fugitive impressions
As we passed, grasped for a moment then sucked away –
Woods, hills, white farms changing shape and position,
A river which wandered, as if not sure of the way,

* A strand on the coast of Co. Mayo where the race was held – also the name of a river.

211

Into and off the pane. A landscape less
Well-groomed than, say, a Florentine painter's one,
But its cross-rhythmed shagginess soothed me through the glass
As it ambled past out there in the setting sun.

Then, one Welsh mead turned up with a girl rider –
Light hair, red jersey – cantering her horse.
Momently creatures out of some mythical order
Of being they seemed, to justify and endorse

A distrait mood . . . I recalled you at thirteen
Matched against Irish farmers in a race
On Carrownisky – under the cap your dark mane
Streaming, the red windcheater a far-off blaze;

But most how, before the race began, you rode
Slowly round the circuit of sand to calm
The mare and accustom her to a lawless crowd.
Seeing that, I knew you should come to no harm.

Our nerves too can taste of our children's pure
Confidence and grow calm. My daughter rides back
To me down that railside field – elemental, secure
As an image that time may bury but not unmake.

CHILDREN LEAVING HOME*

Soon you'll be off to meet your full-grown selves,
Freed from my guardianship to sweat out your own life-sentence.
The house will be emptied of you,
For every tie in time dissolves;
And you, once close to us like a whisper of blood, in due
Season return, if return you will, as polite acquaintance.

* First published posthumously in support of a magazine called *Tagus*.

212

What will you then remember? The lime that crowded
Your bedroom windows, shading the square rose-bed beneath –
All such everyday sights,
Hours by boredom or wrath enclouded,
Or those which burst like a rocket with red-letter delights
In a holiday sky – picnics, the fair on Blackheath?

I heard you last summer, crossing Ireland by road,
Ask the mother to re-tell episodes out of your past.
You gave them the rapt attention
A ballad-maker's audience owed
To fact caught up in fable. Through memory's dimension
The unlikeliest scene may be immortalised.

Forgive my coldnesses, now past recall,
Angers, injustice, moods contrary, mean or blind;
And best, my dears, forgive
Yourselves, when I am gone, for all
Love-signals you ignored and for the fugitive
Openings you never took into my mind.

At that hour what shall I have to bequeath?
A sick world we could not change, a sack of genes
I did not choose, some verse
Long out of fashion, a laurel wreath
Wilted . . . So prematurely our old age inters
Puny triumphs with poignant might-have-beens.

Soon you'll be leaving home, alone to face
Love's treacheries and transports. May these early years
Have shaped you to be whole,
To live unshielded from the rays
Which probe, enlighten and mature the human soul.
Go forth and make the best of it, my dears.

AT LEMMONS*

For Jane, Kingsley, Colin, Sargy with much love

Above my table three magnolia flowers
Utter their silent requiems.
Through the window I see your elms
In labour with the racking storm
Giving it shape in April's shifty airs.

Up there sky boils from a brew of cloud
To blue gleam, sunblast, then darkens again.
No respite is allowed
The watching eye, the natural agony.

Below is the calm a loved house breeds
Where four have come together to dwell
– Two write, one paints, the fourth invents –
Each pursuing a natural bent
But less through nature's formative travail
Than each in his own humour finding the self he needs.

Round me all is amenity, a bloom of
Magnolia uttering its requiems,
A climate of acceptance. Very well
I accept my weakness with my friends'
Good natures sweetening every day my sick room.

---

* This was written on his deathbed. Lemmons was the house at Hadley Common
where CDL died. It was owned then by Elizabeth Jane Howard and Kingsley Amis.
EJH's brother, Colin Howard, the inventor, and the painter, Sargy Mann, also lived
there.

LIST OF SUBSCRIBERS

Juliet Ace
Anthony Arblaster
Jim Armstrong
Norman Ayrton
William Baker
Michael & Melissa Bakewell
Jill Balcon
A. Banerjee
Bedales Memorial Library
Dorreen & Brian Blow
Sue Bolt
John A. B. Bolton
Frances Bond
Lew Bowyer
Julian Bream
Adrian Brett
June & Douglas Brooks
Ashley Brown
Chris Brown
Stuart Bruce
Dawn Bruin
David Burnett
Roy Burton
Diana Carter
Barbara Ann Clark
Pam Clarke
June Colley
Mrs S. Colquhoun
Alan B. Cook
Dr F. B. Cookson
Terence Cooper
Max Craft
Emma A. L. Cranidge
Kevin Crossley-Holland
Martyn Crucefix
Alan Cudmore
Neil Curry
Vanessa Davis
Delos Press
Frank Dickinson, Ilkley Poets

Jonathan Dove & Alasdair
   Middleton
Christopher Dowling
Chris & Margaret Ducker
John Dunne
Jane Duran
Tom Durham
Dianah Ellis
Richard & Liz Emeny
U. A. Fanthorpe & Dr R. V. Bailey
James Fergusson
Duncan Forbes
Eric & Joy Francis
Christopher Fry
Richard Furniss
Valerie A. Gates
Albert & Barbara Gelpi
James Gibson
Robert Gomme
Lawrence Green
Lee Griffin
Frances Guthrie
Martin Haggerty
Steven Halliwell
The Right Reverend Richard
   Harries
S. Harrison
Anne Harvey
Mr & Mrs J. C. Henshaw
John Henton
Dominic Hibberd
Jeremy Hooker
Elizabeth Jane Howard
David Hughes
S. Richard Hutchings
Jeremy Hutchinson
M. C. Hyde
Kit Jackson
Isabel J. Jacob, Oswestry
Terry Johnson

215

Liam Keaveney
Nosheen Khan
Jo Kingham
Chris Langley
Mike Leishman
Roy F. Lewis
Jean P. Liddiard
Alan & Judy Lloyd
Michael Longley
Mrs Jane M. Lowther
Peter Mair
Anne Mallinson
Alan A. Martin
Revd David Mason
Rohinten D. Mazda
Ian McKelvie
Helen McPhail, The Wilfred
    Owen Association
Mr J. B. Meff
Michael Meredith
Gwen Millan
Edward Mirzoeff, CVO, CBE
Adrian Mitchell
Anne Patricia Morgan
Linda Morgan
Stuart Jasper Morgan
James Morwood
Paul Muldoon
Alan Munton
Russell Ogden
Masatsugu Ohtake
Iona Opie
Michael O'Sullivan
Wilfred Owen Association
Richard Packer
Bernard Palmer & Tim Woodward
Richard & Barbara Pasco
Janet Mary Penfold
Menna & Alan Picton
Piers Plowright
Malcolm Porteous
Shahed Power
Dr & Mrs Quick
Isabel Quigly, FRSL
Anthony P. (Tony) Quinn, Dublin
Pamela Rachet
Rainbow Poetry Library, East
    Sussex

Arnold & Simonette Rattenbury
Mike Redhead
Michael J. Reynolds
Irfon Roberts
Ruth Robinson
Audrey Russell-Smith
Barbara Samson
Myra Schneider
Mary Anne Schwalbe
Will Schwalbe
Ruth Shelton
Sherborne School
Laurence Skillman
Daphne V. Skone
Revd M. Southworth Miners
Jon Stallworthy
Peter Stanford
Isabel Bonnyman Stanley &
    Ronald Kelly Giles
Joan Stevens
Michael & Chantal Stokely
Summer Fields School
Pauline Tennant
Hallam Tennyson
Dr David Thomas
Edward C. Thomas
Myfanwy Thomas
C. G. Trotman & Selina Trotman
Rodney Troubridge
Ann & Anthony Thwaite
Douglas & Ruth Vicary
Cecily Marendaz Walker
Graham K. A. Walker
John Walker
Dave Walton
Matthew Waterhouse
Mr & Mrs Max Watson
Len Webster
Brian Hadley Wells
David Whiting
Mrs Austen Williams
David Williams
Tim Williams
Eliane Wilson
Vicki Wilson
Adolf & Dawn Wood
Gabriel Woolf
David Worthington

216